Victoria C. Woodhull (First Female American Presidential Candidate): A Biographical Sketch

And

The Truth Shall Make You Free: A Speech On The Principles Of Social Freedom

Theodore Tilton
Victoria C. Woodhull

**Victoria C. Woodhull (First Female American Presidential
Candidate): A Biographical Sketch And The Truth Shall Make You
Free: A Speech On The Principles Of Social Freedom**

Contact:
BibliotechPress@gmail.com

The present edition is a reproduction of 1871 publication of this work. Minor
typographical errors may have been corrected without note, however, for an
authentic reading experience the spelling, punctuation, and capitalization have
been retained from the original text.

ISBN: 978-1-61895-224-0

Content

MR. TILTON'S ACCOUNT OF MRS. WOODHULL

"He that uttereth a slander is a fool."
—Solomon: Prov. x. 18.

I shall swiftly sketch the life of Victoria Claflin Woodhull; a young woman whose career has been as singular as any heroine's in a romance; whose ability is of a rare and whose character of the rarest type; whose personal sufferings are of themselves a whole drama of pathos; whose name (through the malice of some and the ignorance of others) has caught a shadow in strange contrast with the whiteness of her life; whose position as a representative of her sex in the greatest reform of modern times renders her an object of peculiar interest to her fellow-citizens; and whose character (inasmuch as I know her well) I can portray without color or tinge from any other partiality save that I hold her in uncommon respect.

In Homer, Ohio, in a small cottage, white-painted and high-peaked, with a porch running round it and a flower garden in front, this daughter, the seventh of ten children of Roxana and Buckman Claflin, was born September 23d, 1838. As this was the year when Queen Victoria was crowned, the new-born babe, though clad neither in purple nor fine linen, but comfortably swaddled in respectable poverty, was immediately christened (though without chrism) as the Queen's namesake; her parents little dreaming that their daughter would one day aspire to a higher seat than the English throne. The Queen, with that early matronly predilection which her subsequent life did so much to illustrate, foresaw that many glad mothers, who were to bring babes into the world during that coronation year, would name them after the chief lady of the earth; and accordingly she ordained a gift to all her little namesakes of Anno Domini 1838. As Victoria Claflin was one of these, she has lately been urged to make a trip to Windsor Castle, to see the illustrious giver of these gifts, and to receive the special souvenir which the Queen's bounty is supposed to hold still in store for the Ohio babe that uttered its first cry as if to say "Long live the Queen!" Mrs. Woodhull, who is now a candidate for the Presidency of the United States, should defer this visit till after her election, when she will have a beautiful opportunity to invite her elder sister in sovereignty—the mother of our mother country—to visit her fairest daughter, the Republic of the West.

It is pitiful to be a child without a childhood. Such was she. Not a sunbeam gilded the morning of her life. Her girlish career was a continuous bitterness—an unbroken heart-break. She was worked like a slave—whipped like a convict. Her father was impartial in his cruelty to all his children; her mother, with a fickleness of spirit that renders her one of the most erratic of mortals, sometimes abetted him in his scourgings, and at other times shielded the little ones from his blows. In a barrel of rain-water he kept a number of braided green withes made of willow or walnut twigs, and with these stinging weapons, never with an ordinary whip, he would cut the quivering flesh of the children till their tears and blood melted him into mercy. Sometimes he took a handsaw or a stick of firewood as the instrument of his savagery. Coming home after the children were in bed, on learning of some offence which they had committed, he has been known to waken them out of sleep, and to whip them till morning. In consequence of these brutalities, one of the sons, in his thirteenth year, burst away from home, went to sea, and still bears in a shattered constitution the damning memorial of his father's wrath. "I have no remembrance of a father's kiss," says Victoria. Her mother has on occasions tormented and harried her children until they would be thrown into spasms, whereat she would hysterically laugh, clap her hands, and look as fiercely delighted as a cat in playing with a mouse. At other times, her tenderness toward her offspring would appear almost angelic. She would fondle them, weep over them, lift her arms and thank God for such children, caress them with ecstatic joy, and then smite them as if seeking to destroy at a blow both body and soul. This eccentric old lady, compounded in equal parts of heaven and hell, will pray till her eyes are full of tears, and in the same hour curse till her lips are white with foam. The father exhibits a more tranquil bitterness, with fewer spasms. These parental peculiarities were lately made witnesses against their possessors in a court of justice.

If I must account for what seems unaccountable, I may say that with these parents, these traits are not only constitutional but have been further developed by circumstances. The mother, who has never in her life learned to read, was during her maidenhood the petted heiress of one of the richest German families of Pennsylvania, and was brought up not to serve but to be served, until in her ignorance and vanity she fancied all things her own, and all people her ministers. The father, partly bred to the law and partly to real-estate speculations, early in life acquired affluence, but during Victoria's third year suddenly lost all that he had gained, and sat down like a beggar in the dust of despair. The mother, from her youth, had been a religious monomaniac—a spiritualist before the name of spiritualism was coined, and before the Rochester knockings had noised themselves into the public ear. She saw visions and dreamed dreams. During the half year preceding Victoria's birth, the mother became powerfully excited by a religious revival, and went through the process known as "sanctification." She would rise in prayer-meetings and pour forth passionate hallelujahs that sometimes electrified the worshippers. The father, colder in temperament, yet equally inclined to the supernatural, was her partner in these excitements. When the stroke of poverty felled them to the earth, these exultations were quenched in grief. The father, in the opinion of some, became partially crazed; he would take long and rapid walks, sometimes of twenty miles, and come home with bleeding feet and haggard face. The mother, never wholly sane, would huddle her children together as a hen her chickens, and wringing her hands above them, would pray by the hour that God would protect her little brood. Intense melancholy—a misanthropic gloom thick as a sea-fog—seized jointly upon both their minds, and at intervals ever since has blighted them with its mildew. It is said that a fountain cannot send forth at the same time sweet waters and bitter, and yet affection and enmity will proceed from this couple almost at the same moment. At times, they

4

are full of craftiness, low cunning, and malevolence; at other times, they beam with sunshine, sweetness, and sincerity. I have seen many strange people, but the strangest of all are the two parents whose commingled essence constitutes the spiritual principle of the heroine of this tale.

Just here, if anyone asks, "How is it that such parents should not have reproduced their eccentricities in their children?" I answer, "This is exactly what they have done." The whole brood are of the same feather—except Victoria and Tennie. What language shall describe them? Such another family-circle of cats and kits, with soft fur and sharp claws, purring at one moment and fighting the next, never before filled one house with their clamors since Babel began. They love and hate—they do good and evil—they bless and smite each other. They are a sisterhood of furies, tempered with love's melancholy. Here and there one will drop on her knees and invoke God's vengeance on the rest. But for years there has been one common sentiment sweetly pervading the breasts of a majority towards a minority of the offspring, namely, a determination that Victoria and Tennie should earn all the money for the support of the numerous remainder of the Claflin tribe—wives, husbands, children, servants, and all. Being daughters of the horse-leech, they cry "give." It is the common law of the Claflin clan that the idle many shall eat up the substance of the thrifty few. Victoria is a green leaf, and her legion of relatives are caterpillars who devour her. Their sin is that they return no thanks after meat; they curse the hand that feeds them. They are what my friend Mr. Greeley calls "a bad crowd." I am a little rough in saying this, I admit; but I have a rude prejudice in favor of the plain truth.

Victoria's school-days comprised, all told, less than three years—stretching with broken intervals between her eighth and eleventh. The aptest learner of her class, she was the pet alike of scholars and teacher. Called "The Little Queen" (not only from her name but her demeanor) she bore herself with mimic royalty, like one born to command. Fresh and beautiful, her countenance being famed throughout the neighborhood for its striking spirituality, modest, yet energetic, and restive from the over-fulness of an inward energy such as quickened the young blood of Joan of Arc, she was a child of genius, toil, and grief. The little old head on the little young shoulders was often bent over her school-book at the midnight hour. Outside of the school-room, she was a household drudge, serving others so long as they were awake, and serving herself only when they slept. Had she been born black, or been chained to a cart-wheel in Alabama, she could not have been a more enslaved slave. During these school-years, child as she was, she was the many-burdened maid-of-all-work in the large family of a married sister; she made fires, she washed and ironed, she baked bread, she cut wood, she spaded a vegetable garden, she went on errands, she tended infants, she did everything. "Victoria! Victoria!" was the call in the morning before the cock-crowing; when, bouncing out of bed, the "little steam engine," as she was styled, began her buzzing activities for the day. Light and fleet of step, she ran like a deer. She was everybody's favorite—loved, petted, and by some marveled at as a semi-supernatural being. Only in her own home (not a sweet but bitter home) was she treated with the cruelty that still beclouds the memory of her early days.

I must now let out a secret. She acquired her studies, performed her work, and lived her life by the help (as she believes) of heavenly spirits. From her childhood till now (having reached her thirty-third year) her anticipation of the other world has been more vivid than her realization of this. She has entertained angels, and not unawares. These gracious guests have been her constant companions. They abide with her night and day. They dictate her life with daily revelation; and like St. Paul, she is "not disobedient to the heavenly vision." She goes and comes at their behest. Her enterprises are not the coinage of her own brain, but of their divine invention. Her writings and speeches are the products, not only of their indwelling in her soul, but of their absolute control of her brain and tongue. Like a good Greek of the olden time, she does nothing without consulting her oracles. Never, as she avers, have they deceived her, nor ever will she neglect their decrees. One-third of human life is passed in sleep; and in her case, a goodly fragment of this third is spent in trance. Seldom a day goes by but she enters into this fairy-land, or rather into this spirit-realm. In pleasant weather, she has a habit of sitting on the roof of her stately mansion on Murray Hill, and there communing hour by hour with the spirits. She as a religious devotee—her simple theology being an absorbing faith in God and the angels.

Moreover, I may as well mention here as later, that every characteristic utterance which she gives to the world is dictated while under spirit-influence, and most often in a totally unconscious state. The words that fall from her lips are garnered by the swift pen of her husband, and published almost verbatim as she gets and gives them. To take an illustration, after her recent nomination to the Presidency by "The Victoria League," she sent to that committee a letter of superior dignity and moral weight. It was a composition which she had dictated while so outwardly oblivious to the dictation, that when she ended and awoke, she had no memory at all of what she had just done. The product of that strange and weird mood was a beautiful piece of English, not unworthy of Macaulay; and to prove what I say, I adduce the following eloquent passage, which (I repeat) was published without change as it fell from her unconscious lips:

"I ought not to pass unnoticed," she says, "your courteous and graceful allusion to what you deem the favoring omen of my name. It is true that a Victoria rules the great rival nation opposite to us on the other shore of the Atlantic, and it might grace the amity just sealed between the two nations, and be a new security of peace, if a twin sisterhood of Victorias were to preside over the two nations. It is true, also, that in its mere etymology the name signifies *Victory!* and the victory for the right is what we are bent on securing. It is again true, also, that to some minds there is a consonant harmony between the idea and the word, so that its euphonious utterance seems to their imaginations to be itself a genius of success. However this may be, I have sometimes imagined that there is perhaps something providential and prophetic in the fact that my parents were prompted to confer on me a name which forbids the very thought of failure; and, as the great Napoleon believed the star of his destiny, you will at least excuse me, and charge it to the credulity of the woman, if I believe also in fatality of triumph as somehow inhering in my name."

In quoting this passage, I wish to add that its author is a person of no special literary training; indeed, so averse to the pen that, of her own will, she rarely dips it into ink, except to sign her business autograph; nor would she ever write at all except for those spirit-promptings which she dare not disobey; and she could not possibly have produced the above peroration except by some strange intellectual quickening—some over-brooding moral help. This (as she says) she derives from the spirit-world. One of her texts is, "I will lift up mine eyes unto the hills whence cometh my help—my help cometh from the Lord who made Heaven and Earth." She reminds me of the old engraving of St. Gregory dictating his homilies under the outspread wing of the Holy Dove.

It has been so from her childhood. So that her school studies were, literally, a daily miracle. She would glance at a page, and know it by heart. The tough little mysteries which bother the bewildered brains of country-school dullards were always to her as vivid as the sunshine. And when sent on long and weary errands, she believes that she has been lifted over the ground by her angelic helpers—"lest she should dash her feet against a stone." When she had too heavy a basket to carry, an unseen hand would sometimes carry it for her. Digging in the garden as if her back would break, occasionally a strange restfulness would refresh her, and she knew that the spirits were toiling in her stead. All this may seem an illusion to everybody else, but will never be other than a reality to her.

Let me cite some details of these spiritual phenomena, curious in themselves, and illustrating the forces that impel her career.

"My spiritual vision," she says, "dates back as early as my third year." In Victoria's birth place, a young woman named Rachel Scribner, about twenty-five years of age, who had been Victoria's nurse, suddenly 11died. On the day of her death, Victoria was picked up by her departing spirit, and borne off into the spirit-world. To this day Mrs. Woodhull describes vividly her childish sensations as she felt herself gliding through the air—like St. Catharine winged away by the angels. Her mother testifies that while this scene was enacting to the child's inner consciousness, her little body lay as if dead for three hours.

Two of her sisters, who had died in childhood, were constantly present with her. She would talk to them as a girl tattles to her dolls. They were her most fascinating playmates, and she never cared for any others while she had their invisible society.

In her tenth year, one day while sitting by the side of a cradle rocking a sick babe to sleep, she says that two angels came, and gently pushing her away, began to fan the child with their white hands, until its face grew fresh and rosy. Her mother then suddenly entered the chamber, and beheld in amazement the little nurse lying in a trance on the floor, her face turned upward toward the ceiling, and the pining babe apparently in the bloom of health.

The chief among her spiritual visitants, and one who has been a majestic guardian to her from the earliest years of her remembrance, she describes as a matured man of stately figure, clad in a Greek tunic, solemn and graceful in his aspect, strong in his influence, and altogether dominant over her life. For many years, notwithstanding an almost daily visit to her vision, he withheld his name, nor would her most importunate questionings induce him to utter it. But he always promised that in due time he would reveal his identity. Meanwhile he prophecied to her that she would rise to great distinction; that she would emerge from her poverty and live in a stately house; that she would win great wealth in a city which he pictured as crowded with ships; that she would publish and conduct a journal; and that finally, to crown her career, she would become the ruler of her people. At length, after patiently waiting on this spirit-guide for twenty years, one day in 1868, during a temporary sojourn in Pittsburgh, and while she was sitting at a marble table, he suddenly appeared to her, and wrote on the table in English letters the name "Demosthenes." At first the writing was indistinct, but grew to such a luster that the brightness filled the room. The apparition, familiar as it had been before, now affrighted her to trembling. The stately and commanding spirit told her to journey to New York, where she would find at No. 17 Great Jones street a house in readiness for her, equipped in all things to her use and taste. She unhesitatingly obeyed, although she never before had heard of Great Jones street, nor until that revelatory moment had

11

entertained an intention of taking such a residence. On entering the house, it fulfilled in reality the picture which she saw of it in her vision—the self-same hall, stairways, rooms, and furniture. Entering with some bewilderment into the library, she reached out her hand by chance, and without knowing what she did, took up a book which, on idly looking at its title, she saw (to her blood-chilling astonishment) to be "The Orations of Demosthenes." From that time onward, the Greek statesman has been even more palpably than in her earlier years her prophetic monitor, mapping out the life which she must follow, as a chart for a ship sailing the sea. She believes him to be her familiar spirit—the author of her public policy, and the inspirer of her published words. Without intruding my own opinion as to the authenticity of this inspiration, I have often thought that if Demosthenes could arise and speak English, he could hardly excel the fierce light and heat of some of the sentences which I have heard from this singular woman in her glowing hours.

I now turn back to her first marriage. The bride (pitiful to tell) was in her fourteenth year, the bridegroom in his twenty-eighth. It was a fellowship of misery—and her parents, who abetted it, ought to have prevented it. The Haytians speak of escaping out of the river by leaping into the sea. From the endurable cruelty of her parents, she fled to the unendurable cruelty of her husband. She had been from her twelfth to her fourteenth year a double victim, first to chills and fever, and then to rheumatism, which had jointly played equal havoc with her beauty and health, until she was brought within a step of "the iron door." Dr. Canning Woodhull, a gay rake, but whose habits were kept hid from *her* under the general respectability of his family connections (his father being an eminent judge, and his uncle the mayor of New York), was professionally summoned to visit the child, and being a trained physician arrested her decline. Something about her artless manners and vivacious mind captivated his fancy. Coming as a prince, he found her as Cinderella—a child of the ashes. Before she entirely recovered, and while looking haggard and sad, one day he stopped her in the street, and said, "My little chick, I want you to go with me to the pic-nic"—referring to a projected Fourth of July excursion then at hand. The promise of a little pleasure acted like a charm on the house-worn and sorrow-stricken child. She obtained her mother's assent to her going, but her father coupled it with the condition that she should first earn money enough to buy herself a pair of shoes. So the little fourteen-year-old drudge became for the nonce an apple-merchant, and with characteristic business energy sold her apples and bought her shoes. She went to the pic-nic with Dr. Woodhull, like a ticket-of-leave juvenile-delinquent on a furlough. On coming home from the festival, the brilliant fop who, tired of the demi-monde ladies whom he could purchase for his pleasure, and inspired with a sudden and romantic interest in this artless maid, said to her, "My little puss, tell your father and mother that I want you for a wife." The startled girl quivered with anger at this announcement, and with timorous speed fled to her mother and repeated the tale, feeling as if some injury was threatened her, and some danger impended. But the parents, as if not unwilling to be rid of a daughter whose sorrow was ripening her into a woman before her time, were delighted at the unexpected offer. They thought it a grand match. They helped the young man's suit, and augmented their persecutions of the child. Ignorant, innocent, and simple, the girl's chief thought of the proffered marriage was as an escape from the parental yoke. Four months later she accepted the change—flying from the ills she had to others that she knew not of. Her captor, once possessed of his treasure, ceased to value it. On the third night after taking his child-wife to his lodgings, he broke her heart by remaining away all night at a house of ill-repute. Then for the first time she learned, to her dismay, that he was habitually unchaste, and given to long fits of intoxication. She was stung to the quick. The shock awoke all her womanhood. She grew ten years older in a single day. A tumult of thoughts swept like a whirlwind through her mind, ending at last in one predominant purpose, namely, to reclaim her husband. She set herself religiously to this pious task—calling on God and the spirits to help her in it.

Six weeks after her marriage (during which time her husband was mostly with his cups and his mistresses), she discovered a letter addressed to him in a lady's elegant penmanship, saying, "Did you marry that child because she too was *en famille*?" This was an additional thunderbolt. The fact was that her husband, on the day of his marriage, had sent away into the country a mistress who a few months later gave birth to a child.

Squandering his money like a prodigal, he suddenly put his wife into the humblest quarters, where, left mostly to herself, she dwelt in bitterness of spirit, aggravated from time to time by learning of his ordering baskets of champagne and drinking himself drunk in the company of harlots.

Sometimes, with uncommon courage, through rain and sleet, half clad and shivering, she would track him to his dens, and by the energy of her spirit compel him to return. At other times, all night long she would watch at the window, waiting for his footsteps, until she heard them languidly shuffling along the pavement with the staggering reel of a drunken man, in the shameless hours of the morning.

During all this time, she passionately prayed Heaven to give her the heart of her husband, but Heaven, decreeing otherwise, withheld it from her, and for her good.

In fifteen months after her marriage, while living in a little low frame-house in Chicago, in the dead of winter, with icicles clinging to her bed-post, and attended only by her half-drunken husband, she brought forth in almost mortal agony her first-born child. In her ensuing helplessness, she became an object of pity to a next-door neighbor who, with a kindness which the sufferer's unhomelike home did not afford, brought her day by day some nourishing dish. This same ministering hand would then wrap the babe in a blanket, and take it to a happier mother in the near neighborhood, who was at the same time nursing a new-born son. In this way Victoria and her child—themselves both children—were cared for with mingled gentleness and neglect.

At the end of six days, the little invalid attempted to rise and put her sick-room in order, when she was taken with delirium, during which her mother visited her just in time to save her life.

On her recovery, and after a visit to her father's house, she returned to her own to be horror-struck at discovering that her bed had been occupied the night before by her husband in company with a wanton of the streets, and that the room was littered with the remains of their drunken feast.

Once, after a month's desertion by him, until she had no money and little to eat, she learned that he was keeping a mistress at a fashionable boarding-house, under the title of wife. The true wife, still wrestling with God for the renegade, sallied forth into the wintry street, clad in a calico dress without undergarments, and shod only with india-rubbers without shoes or stockings, entered the house, confronted the household as they sat at table, told her story to the confusion of the paramour and his mistress, and drew tears from all the company till, by a common movement, the listeners compelled the harlot to pack her trunk and flee the city, and shamed the husband into creeping like a spaniel back into the kennel which his wife still cherished as her home.

To add to her misery, she discovered that her child, begotten in drunkenness, and born in squalor, was a half idiot; predestined to be a hopeless imbecile for life; endowed with just enough intelligence to exhibit the light of reason in dim eclipse:—a sad and pitiful spectacle in his mother's house to-day, where he roams from room to room, muttering noises more sepulchral than human; a daily agony to the woman who bore him, hoping more of her burden; and heightening the pathos of the perpetual scene by the uncommon sweetness of his temper which, by winning every one's love, doubles every one's pity.

Journeying to California as a region where she might inspire her husband to begin a new life freed from old associations, she there found herself and her little family strangers in a strange city—beggars in a land of plenty. Change of sky is not change of mind. Dr. Woodhull took his habits, his wife took her necessities, and both took their misery, from East to West. In San Francisco, the girlish woman, with unrelaxed energy, and as part of that life-long heroism which will one day have its monument, set herself to supporting the man by whom she ought to have been supported. A morning journal had an advertisement—"A cigar girl wanted." The wife, with her face of sweet sixteen, presented herself as the first candidate, and was accepted on the spot. The proprietor was a stalwart Californian—one of those men who catch from a new country something of the liberality which the sailor brings from the sea. She served for one day behind his counter—blushing, modest, and sensitive, her ears tingling at every rude remark by every uncouth customer—and at nightfall her employer, who had noticed the blood coming and going in her cheeks, said to her, "My little lady, you are not the clerk I want; I must have somebody who can rough it; you are too fine." Inquiring into her case, he was surprised to find her married and a mother. At first he discredited this information, but there was no denying the truth of her story. He accompanied her to her husband, and as the two men discovered themselves to each other as brother free-masons, he gave his fair clerk of a day a twenty-dollar gold piece, and dismissed her with his blessing. And I hope this has been revisited on his own head.

Resorting to her needle, she carried from house to house this only weapon which many women possess wherewith to fight the battle of life. She chanced to come upon Anna Cogswell, the actress, who wanted a seamstress to make her a theatrical wardrobe. The winsome dressmaker was engaged at once. But her earnings at this new calling did not keep pace with her expenses. "It is no use," said she to her dramatic friend; "I am running behindhand. I must do something better." "Then," replied the actress, "you too must be an actress." And, nothing loth to undertake anything new and difficult, Victoria, who never before had dreamed of such a possibility, was engaged as a lesser light to the Cogswell star. For a first appearance, she was cast in the part of the "Country Cousin" in "New York by Gaslight." The text was given to her in the morning, she learned and rehearsed it during the day, and made a fair hit in it at night. For six weeks thereafter, she earned fifty-two dollars a week as an actress.

"Never leave the stage," said some of her fellow-performers, all of whom admired her simplicity and spirituality. "But I do not care for the stage," she said, "and I shall leave it at the first opportunity. I am meant for some other fate. But what it is, I know not."

It came—as all things have came to her—through the agency of spirits. One night while on the boards, clad in a pink silk dress and slippers, acting in the ballroom scene in the "Corsican Brothers," suddenly a spirit-voice addressed her, saying, "Victoria, come home!" Thrown instantly into clairvoyant condition, she saw a vision of her young sister Tennie, then a mere child—standing by her mother, and both calling the absent one to return. Her mother and Tennie were then in Columbus, Ohio. She saw Tennie distinctly enough to notice that she wore a striped French calico frock. "Victoria come home!" said the little messenger, beckoning with her childish forefinger. The apparition would not be denied. Victoria, thrilled and chilled by the vision and voice, burst away at a bound behind the scenes, and without waiting to change her dress, ran, clad with all her dramatic adornments, through a foggy rain to her hotel, and packing up her few things that night, betook herself with her husband and child next morning to the steamer bound for New York. On the voyage she was thrown into such vivid spiritual states, that she produced a profound excitement among the passengers. On reaching her mother's home, she came upon Tennie dressed in the same dress as in the vision; and on inquiring the meaning of the message, "Victoria, come home!" was told that at the time it was uttered, her mother had said to Tennie, "My dear, send the spirits after Victoria to bring her home;" and moreover the French calico dress had appeared to her spirit-sight at the very first moment its wearer had put it on.

This homeward trip, and its consequences, marked a new phase in her career—a turning point in her life.

Hitherto her clairvoyant faculty had been put to no pecuniary use, but she was now directed by the spirits to repair to Indianapolis, there to announce herself as a medium, and to treat patients for the cure of disease. Taking rooms in the Bates House, and publishing a card in the journals, she found herself able, on saluting her callers, to tell by inspiration their names, their residences, and their maladies. In a few days she became the town's talk. Her marvellous performances in clairvoyance being noised abroad, people flocked to her from a distance. Her rooms were crowded and her purse grew fat. She reaped a golden harvest—including, as its worthiest part, golden opinions from all sorts of people. Her countenance would often glow as with a sacred light, and she became an object of religious awe to many wonder-stricken people whose inward lives she had revealed. Moreover, her unpretentious modesty, and her perpetual disclaimer of any merit or power of her own, and the entire crediting of this to spirit-influence, augmented the interest with which all spectators regarded the amiable prodigy. First at Indianapolis, and afterward at Terre Haute, she wrought some apparently miraculous cures. She straightened the feet of the lame; she opened the ears of the deaf; she detected the robbers of a bank; she brought to light hidden crimes; she solved physiological problems; she unveiled business secrets; she prophecied future events. Knowing the wonders which she wrought, certain citizens disguised themselves and came to her purporting to be strangers from a distant town, but she instantly said, "Oh, no; you all live here." "How can you tell?" they asked. "The spirits say so," she replied.

Benedictions followed her; gifts were lavished upon her; money flowed in a stream toward her. Journeying from city to city in the practice of her spiritual art, she thereby supported all her relatives far and near. Her income in one year reached nearly a hundred thousand dollars. She received in one day, simply as fees for cures which she had wrought, five thousand dollars. The sum total of the receipts of her practice, and of her investments growing out of it, up to the time of its discontinuance by direction of the spirits in 1869, was $700,000. The age of wonders has not ceased!

During all this period, though outwardly prosperous, she was inwardly wretched. The dismal fact of her son's half-idiocy so preyed upon her mind that, in a heat of morbid feeling, she fell to accusing her innocent self for his misfortunes. The sight of his face rebuked her, until, in brokenness of spirit, she prayed to God for another child—a daughter, to be born with a fair body and a sound mind. Her prayer was granted, but not without many accompaniments of inhumanity. Once during her carriage of her unborn charge, she was kicked by its father in a fit of drunkenness—inflicting a bruise on her body and a greater bruise to her spirit. Profound as her double suffering was, in its lowest depth there was a deeper still. She was plunged into this at the child's birth. This event occurred at No. 53 Bond Street, New York, April 23d, 1861. She and her husband were at the time the only occupants of the house—her trial coming upon her while no nurse, or servant, or other human helper was under the roof. The babe entered the world at four o'clock in the morning, handled by the feverish and unsteady hands of its intoxicated father, who, only half in possession of his professional skill, cut the umbilical cord too near the flesh and tied it so loose that the string came off—laid the babe in its mother's arms—in an hour afterward left them asleep and alone—and then staggered out of the house. Nor did he remember to return. Meanwhile, the mother, on waking, was startled to find that her head on the side next to her babe's body was in a pool of blood—that her hair was soaked and clotted in a little red stream oozing drop by drop from the bowels of the child. In her motherly agony, reaching a broken chair-rung which happened to be lying near, she pounded against the wall to summon help from the next house. At intervals for several hours she continued this pounding, no one answering—until at length one of the neighbors, a resolute woman, who was attracted toward the noise, but unable to get in at the front-door, removed the grating of the basement, and made her way up stairs to the rescue of the mother and her babe. On the third day after, the mother, on sitting propped in her bed and looking out of the window, caught sight of her husband staggering up the steps of a house across the way, mistaking it for his own!

It was this horrible experience that first awoke her mind to the question, "Why should I any longer live with this man?" Hitherto she had entertained an almost superstitious idea of the devotion with which a wife should cling to her husband. She had always been so faithful to him that, in his cups, he would mock and jeer at her fidelity, and call her a fool for maintaining it. At length the fool grew wiser, and after eleven years of what, with conventional mockery, was called a marriage—during which time her husband had never spent an evening with her at home, had seldom drawn a sober breath, and had spent on other women, not herself, all the money he had ever earned—she applied in Chicago for a divorce, and obtained it.

Previous to this crisis, there had occurred a remarkable incident which more than ever confirmed her faith in the guardianship of spirits. One day, during a severe illness of her son, she left him to visit her patients, and on her return was startled with the news that the boy had died two hours before. "No," she exclaimed, "I will not permit his death." And with frantic energy she stripped her bosom naked, caught up his lifeless form, pressed it to her own, and sitting thus, flesh to flesh, glided insensibly into a trance in which she remained seven hours; at the end of which time she awoke, a perspiration started from his clammy skin, and the child that had been thought dead was brought back again to life—and lives to this day in sad half-death. It is her belief that the spirit of Jesus Christ brooded over the lifeless form, and re-wrought the miracle of Lazarus for a sorrowing woman's sake.

Victoria's father and mother, growing still more fanatical with their advancing years, had all along subjected her to a series of singular vexations. And the elder sisters had joined in the mischief-making, outdoing the parents. Sometimes they would burst in upon Mrs. Woodhull's house, and attempt to govern its internal economy; sometimes they would carry off the furniture, or garments, or pictures; sometimes they would crown her with eulogies as the greatest of human beings, and in the same breath defame her as an agent of the devil.

But their great cause of persecution grew out of her younger sister Tennie's career. This young woman developed, while a child in her father's house, a similar power to Victoria's. It was a penetrating spiritual insight applied to the cure of disease. But her father and mother, who regarded their daughter in the light of the damsel mentioned in the Acts of the Apostles, who "brought her masters much gain by soothsaying," put her before the public as a fortune-teller. By adding to much that was genuine in her mediumship more that was charlatanry, they aroused against this fraudulent business the indignation of the sincere soul of Victoria who, more than most human beings, scorns a lie, and would burn at the stake rather than practise a deceit. She clutched Tennie as by main force and flung her out of this semi-humbug, to the mingled astonishment of her money-greedy family, one and all. At this time Tennie was supporting a dozen or twenty relatives by her ill-gotten gains. Victoria's rescue of her excited the wrath of all these parasites— which has continued hot and undying against both to this day. The fond and fierce mother alternately loves and hates the two united defiers of her morbid will; and the father, at times a Mephistopheles, waits till the inspiration of cunning overmasters his parental instinct, and watching for a moment when his ill word to a stranger will blight their business schemes, drops in upon some capitalist whose money is in their hands, lodges an indictment against his own flesh and blood, takes out his handkerchief to hide a few well-feigned tears, clasps his hands with an unfelt agony, hobbles off smiling sardonically at the mischief which he has done, and the next day repents his wickedness with genuine contrition and manlier woe. These parents would cheerfully give their lives as a sacrifice to atone for the many mischiefs which they have cast like burrs at their children; but if all the scars which they and their progeny have inflicted on one another could be magically healed to-day, they would be scratched open by the same hands and set stinging and tingling anew to-morrow.

There is a maxim that marriages are made in heaven, albeit contradicted by the Scripture which declares that in heaven there is neither marrying nor giving in marriage. But, even against the Scripture, it is safe to say that Victoria's second marriage was made in Heaven; that is, it was decreed by the self-same spirits whom she is ever ready to follow, whether they lead her for discipline into the valley of the shadow of death, or for comfort in those ways of pleasantness which are paths of peace. Col. James H. Blood, commander of the 6th Missouri Regiment, who at the close of the war was elected City Auditor of St. Louis, who became President of the Society of Spiritualists in that place, and who had himself been, like Victoria, the legal partner of a morally sundered marriage, called one day on Mrs. Woodhull to consult her as a spiritualistic physician (having never met her before), and was startled to see her pass into a trance, during which she announced, unconsciously to herself, that his future destiny was to be linked with hers in marriage. Thus, to their mutual amazement, but to their subsequent happiness, they were betrothed on the spot by "the powers of the air." The legal tie by which at first they bound themselves to each other was afterward by mutual consent annulled—the necessary form of Illinois law being complied with to this effect. But the marriage stands on its merits, and is to all who witness its harmony known to be a sweet and accordant union of congenial souls.

Col. Blood is a man of a philosophic and reflective cast of

mind, an enthusiastic student of the higher lore of spiritualism, a recluse from society, and an expectant believer in a stupendous destiny for Victoria. A modesty not uncommon to men of intellect prompts him to sequester his name in the shade rather than to set it glittering in the sun. But he is an indefatigable worker— driving his pen through all hours of the day and half of the night. He is an active editor of *Woodhull & Claflin's Weekly*, and one of the busy partners in the firm of Woodhull, Claflin & Co., Brokers, at Broad street, New York. His civic views are (to use his favorite designation of them) cosmopolitical; in other words, he is a radical of extreme radicalism—an internationalist of the most uncompromising type—a communist who would rather have died in Paris than be the president of a pretended republic whose first official act has been the judicial murder of the only republicans in France. His spiritualistic habits he describes in a letter to his friend, the writer of this memorial, as follows: "At about eleven or twelve o'clock at night, two or three times a week, and sometimes without nightly interval, Victoria and I hold parliament with the spirits. It is by this kind of study that we both have learned nearly all the valuable knowledge that we possess. Victoria goes into a trance, during which her guardian spirit takes control of her mind, speaking audibly through her lips, propounding various matters for our subsequent investigation and verification, and announcing principles, detached thoughts, hints of systems, and suggestions for affairs. In this way, and in this spiritual night-school, began that process of instruction by which Victoria has risen to her present position as a political economist and politician. During her entranced state, which generally lasts about an hour, but sometimes twice as long, I make copious notes of all she says, and when her speech is unbroken, I write down every word, and publish it without correction or amendment. She and I regard all the other portion of our lives as almost valueless compared with these midnight hours." The preceding extract shows that this fine-grained transcendentalist is a reverent husband to his spiritual wife, the sympathetic companion of her entranced moods, and their faithful historian to the world.

After her union with Col. Blood, instead of changing her name to his, she followed the example of many actresses, singers, and other professional women whose names have become a business property to their owners, and she still continues to be known as Mrs. Woodhull.

One night, about half a year after their marriage, she and her husband were wakened at midnight in Cincinnati by the announcement that a man by the name of Dr. Woodhull had been attacked with delirium tremens at the Burnet House, and in a lucid moment had spoken of the woman from whom he had been divorced, and begged to see her. Col. Blood immediately took a carriage, drove to the hotel, brought the wretched victim home, and jointly with Victoria took care of him with life-saving kindness for six weeks. On his going away they gave him a few hundred dollars of their joint property to make him comfortable in another city. He departed full of gratitude, bearing with him the assurance that he would always be welcome to come and go as a friend of the family. And from that day to this, the poor man, dilapidated in body and emasculated in spirit, has sometimes sojourned under Victoria's roof and sometimes elsewhere, according to his whim or will. In the present ruins of the young gallant of twenty years ago, there is more manhood (albeit an expiring spark like a candle at its socket) than during any of the former years; and to be now turned out of doors by the woman whom he wronged, but who would not wrong him in return, would be an act of inhumanity which it would be impossible for Mrs. Woodhull and Col. Blood either jointly or separately to commit. For this piece of noble conduct—what is commonly called her living with two husbands under one roof—she has received not so much censure on earth as I think she will receive reward in heaven. No other passage of her life more signally illustrates the nobility of her moral judgments, or the supernal courage with which she stands by her convictions. Not all the clamorous tongues in Christendom, though they should simultaneously cry out against her "Fie, for shame!" could persuade her to turn this wretched wreck from her home. And I say she is right; and I will maintain this opinion against the combined Pecksniffs of the whole world.

This act, and the malice of enemies, together with her bold opinions on social questions, have combined to give her reputation a stain. But no slander ever fell on any human soul with greater injustice. A more unsullied woman does not walk the earth. She carries in her very face the fair legend of a character kept pure by a sacred fire within. She is one of those aspiring devotees who tread the earth merely as a stepping-stone to Heaven, and whose chief ambition is finally to present herself at the supreme tribunal "spotless, and without wrinkle, or blemish, or any such thing." Knowing her as well as I do, I cannot hear an accusation against her without recalling Tennyson's line of King Arthur,

"Is thy white blamelessness accounted blame?"

Fulfilling a previous prophecy, and following a celestial mandate, in 1869 she founded a bank and published a journal. These two events took the town by storm. When the doors of her office in Broad street were first thrown open to the public, several thousand visitors came in a flock on the first day. The "lady brokers," as they were called (a strange confession that brokers are not always gentlemen) were besieged like lionesses in a cage. The daily press interviewed them; the weekly wits satirized them; the comic sheets caricatured them; but like a couple of fresh young dolphins, breasting the sea side by side, they showed themselves native to the element, and cleft gracefully every threatening wave that broke over their heads. The breakers could not dash the brokers. Indomitable in their energy, the sisters won the good graces of Commodore Vanderbilt—a fine old gentleman of comfortable means, who of all the lower animals prefers the horse, and of all the higher virtues admires pluck. Both with and without Commodore Vanderbilt's help, Mrs. Woodhull has more than once shown the pluck that has held the rein of the stock market as the Commodore holds his horse. Her journal, as one sees it week by week, is generally a willow-basket full of audacious manuscripts, apparently picked up at random and thrown together pell-mell, stunning the reader with a medley of politics, finance, free-love, and the pantarchy. This sheet, when the divinity that shapes its ends shall begin to add to the rough-hewing a little smooth-shaping; in other words, when its unedited chaos shall come to be moulded by the spirits to that order which is Heaven's first law; this not ordinary but "cardinary" journal, which is edited in one world, and published in another, will become less a confusion to either, and more a power for both.

In 1870, following the English plan of self-nomination, Mrs. Woodhull announced herself as a candidate for the Presidency—mainly for the purpose of drawing public attention to the claims of woman to political equality with man. She accompanied this announcement with a series of papers in the *Herald* on politics and finance, which have since been collected into a volume entitled "The Principles of Government." She has lately received a more formal nomination to that high office by "The Victoria League," an organization which, being somewhat Jacobinical in its secrecy, is popularly supposed, though not definitely known, to be presided over by Commodore Vanderbilt, who is also similarly imagined to be the golden corner-stone of the business house of Woodhull, Claflin & Co. Should she be elected to the high seat to which she aspires, (an event concerning which I make no prophecy,) I am at least sure that she would excel any Queen now on any throne in her native faculty to govern others.

One night in December, 1869, while she lay in deep sleep, her Greek guardian came to her, and sitting transfigured by her couch, wrote on a scroll (so that she could not only see the words, but immediately dictated them to her watchful amanuensis) the memorable document now known in history as "The Memorial of Victoria C. Woodhull"—a petition addressed to Congress, claiming under the Fourteenth Amendment the right of women as of other "citizens of the United States" to vote in "the States wherein they reside"—asking, moreover, that the State of New York, of which she was a citizen, should be restrained by Federal authority from preventing her exercise of this constitutional right. As up to this time neither she nor her husband had been greatly interested in woman suffrage, he had no sooner written this manifesto from her lips, than he awoke her from the trance, and protested against the communication as nonsense, believing it to be a trick of some evil-disposed spirits. In the morning the document was shown to a number of friends, including one eminent judge, who ridiculed its logic and conclusions. But the lady herself, from whose sleeping and yet unsleeping brain the strange document had sprung like Minerva from the head of Jove, simply answered that her antique instructor, having never misled her before, was guiding her aright then. Nothing doubting, but much wondering, she took the novel demand to Washington, where, after a few days of laughter from the shallow-minded, and of neglect from the indifferent, it suddenly burst upon the Federal Capitol like a storm, and then spanned it like a rainbow. She went before the Judiciary Committee, and delivered an argument in support of her claim to the franchise under the new Amendments, which some who heard it pronounced one of the ablest efforts which they had ever heard on any subject. She caught the listening ears of Senator Carpenter, Gen. Butler, Judge Woodward, George W. Julian, Gen. Ashley, Judge Loughridge, and other able statesmen in Congress, and harnessed these gentlemen as steeds to her chariot. Such was the force of her appeal that the whole city rushed together to hear it, like the Athenians to the market-place when Demosthenes stood in his own and not a borrowed clay. A great audience, one of the finest ever gathered in the capital, assembled to hear her defend her thesis in the first public speech of her life. At the moment of rising, her face was observed to be very pale, and she appeared about to faint. On being afterward questioned as to the cause of her emotion, she replied that, during the first prolonged moment, she remembered an early prediction of her guardian-spirit, until then forgotten, that she would one day speak in public, and that her first discourse would be pronounced in the capital of her country. The sudden fulfilment of this prophecy smote her so violently that for a moment she was stunned into apparent unconsciousness. But she recovered herself, and passed through the ordeal with great success—which is better luck than happened to the real Demosthenes, for Plutarch mentions that his maiden speech was a failure, and that he was laughed at by the people.

Assisted by Elizabeth Cady Stanton, Paulina Wright Davis, Isabella Beecher Hooker, Susan B. Anthony, and other staunch and able women whom she swiftly persuaded into accepting this construction of the Constitution, she succeeded, after her petition was denied by a majority of the Judiciary Committee, in obtaining a minority report in its favor, signed jointly by Gen. Benj. F. Butler of Massachusetts and Judge Loughridge of Iowa. To have clutched this report from Gen. Butler—as it were a scalp from the ablest head in the House of Representatives—was a sufficient trophy to entitle the brave lady to an enrolment in the political history of her country. She means to go to Washington again next winter to knock at the half-opened doors of the Capitol until they shall swing wide enough asunder to admit her enfranchised sex.

I must say something of her personal appearance although it defies portrayal, whether by photograph or pen. Neither tall nor short, stout nor slim, she is of medium stature, lithe and elastic, free and graceful. Her side face, looked at over her left shoulder, is of perfect aquiline outline, as classic as ever went into a Roman marble, and resembles the masque of Shakespeare taken after death; the same view, looking from the right, is a little broken and irregular; and the front face is broad, with prominent cheek bones, and with some unshapely nasal lines. Her countenance is never twice alike, so variable is its expression and so dependent on her moods. Her soul comes into it and goes out of it, giving her at one time the look of a superior and almost saintly intelligence, and at another leaving her dull, commonplace, and unprepossessing. When under a strong spiritual influence, a strange and mystical light irradiates from her face, reminding the beholder of the Hebrew Lawgiver who gave to men what he received from God and whose face during the transfer shone. Tennyson, as with the hand of a gold-beater, has beautifully gilded the same expression in his stanza of St. Stephen the Martyr in the article of death:

"And looking upward, full of grace,
He prayed, and from a happy place,
God's glory smote him on the face."

33

In conversation, until she is somewhat warmed with earnestness, she halts, as if her mind were elsewhere, but the moment she brings all her faculties to her lips for the full utterance of her message, whether it be of persuasion or indignation, and particularly when under spiritual control, she is a very orator for eloquence—pouring forth her sentences like a mountain stream, sweeping away everything that frets its flood.

Her hair which, when left to itself is as long as those tresses of Hortense in which her son Louis Napoleon used to play hide-and-seek, she now mercilessly cuts close like a boy's, from impatience at the daily waste of time in suitably taking care of this prodigal gift of nature.

She can ride a horse like an Indian, and climb a tree like an athlete; she can swim, row a boat, play billiards, and dance; moreover, as the crown of her physical virtues, she can walk all day like an Englishwoman.

"Difficulties," says Emerson, "exist to be surmounted." This might be the motto of her life. In her lexicon (which is still of youth) there is no such word as fail. Her ambition is stupendous—nothing is too great for her grasp. Prescient of the grandeur of her destiny, she goes forward with a resistless fanaticism to accomplish it. Believing thoroughly in herself (or rather not in herself but in her spirit-aids) she allows no one else to doubt either her or them. In her case the old miracle is enacted anew—the faith which removes mountains. A soul set on edge is a conquering weapon in the battle of life. Such, and of Damascus temper, is hers.

In making an epitome of her views, I may say that in politics she is a downright democrat, scorning to divide her fellow-citizens into upper and lower classes, but ranking them all in one comprehensive equality of right, privilege, and opportunity; concerning finance, which is a favorite topic with her, she holds that gold is not the true standard of money-value, but that the government should abolish the gold-standard, and issue its notes instead, giving to these a fixed and permanent value, and circulating them as the only money; on social questions, her theories are similar to those which have long been taught by John Stuart Mill and Elizabeth Cady Stanton, and which are styled by some as free-love doctrines, while others reject this appellation on account of its popular association with the idea of a promiscuous intimacy between the sexes—the essence of her system being that marriage is of the heart and not of the law, that when love ends marriage should end with it, being dissolved by nature, and that no civil statute should outwardly bind two hearts which have been inwardly sundered; and finally, in religion, she is a spiritualist of the most mystical and ethereal type.

In thus speaking of her views, I will add to them another fundamental article of her creed, which an incident will best illustrate. Once a sick woman who had been given up by the physicians, and who had received from a Catholic priest extreme unction in expectation of death, was put into the care of Mrs. Woodhull, who attempted to lure her back to life. This zealous physician, unwilling to be baffled, stood over her patient day and night, neither sleeping nor eating for ten days and nights, at the end of which time she was gladdened not only at

35

witnessing the sick woman's recovery, but at finding that her own body, instead of weariness or exhaustion from the double lack of sleep and food, was more fresh and bright than at the beginning. Her face, during this discipline, grew uncommonly fair and ethereal; her flesh wore a look of transparency; and the ordinary earthiness of mortal nature began to disappear from her physical frame and its place to be supplied with what she fancied were the foretokens of a spiritual body. These phenomena were so vivid to her own consciousness and to the observation of her friends, that she was led to speculate profoundly on the transformation from our mortal to our immortal state, deducing the idea that the time will come when the living human body, instead of ending in death by disease, and dissolution in the grave, will be gradually refined away until it is entirely sloughed off, and the soul only, and not the flesh, remains. It is in this way that she fulfils to her daring hope the prophecy that "The last enemy that shall be destroyed is death."

Engrossed in business affairs, nevertheless at any moment she would rather die than live—such is her infinite estimate of the other world over this. But she disdains all commonplace parleyings with the spirit-realm such as are had in ordinary spirit-manifestations. On the other hand, she is passionately eager to see the spirits face to face—to summon them at her will and commune with them at her pleasure. Twice (as she unshakenly believes) she has seen a vision of Jesus Christ—honored thus doubly over St. Paul, who saw his Master but once, and then was overcome by the sight. She never goes to any church—save to the solemn temple whose starry arch spans her housetop at night, where she sits like Simeon Stylites on his pillar, a worshipper in the sky. Against the inculcations of her childish education, the spirits have taught her that he whom the church calls the Saviour of the world is not God but man. But her reverence for him is supreme and ecstatic. The Sermon on the Mount fills her eyes with tears. The exulting exclamations of the Psalmist are her familiar outbursts of devotion. For two years, as a talisman against any temptation toward untruthfulness (which, with her, is the unpardonable sin), she wore, stitched into the sleeve of every one of her dresses, the 2d verse of the 120th Psalm, namely, "Deliver my soul, O Lord, from lying lips, and from a deceitful tongue." Speaking the truth punctiliously, whether in great things or small, she so rigorously exacts the same of others, that a deceit practised upon her enkindles her soul to a flame of fire; and she has acquired a clairvoyant or intuitive power to detect a lie in the moment of its utterance, and to smite the liar in his act of guilt. She believes that intellectual power has its fountains in spiritual inspiration. And once when I put to her the searching question, "What is the greatest truth that has ever been expressed in words?" she thrilled me with the sudden answer, "Blessed are the pure in heart for they shall see God."

As showing that her early clairvoyant power still abides, I will mention a fresh instance. An eminent judge in Pennsylvania, in whose court-house I had once lectured, called lately to see me at the office of The Golden Age. On my inquiring after his family, he told me that a strange event had just happened in it. "Three months ago," said he, "while I was in New York, Mrs. Woodhull said to me, with a rush of feeling, 'Judge, I foresee that you will lose two of your children within six weeks.'" This announcement, he said, wounded him as a tragic sort of trifling with life and death. "But," I asked, "did anything follow the prophecy?" "Yes," he replied, "fulfilment; I lost two children within six weeks." The Judge, who is a Methodist, thinks that Victoria the clairvoyant is like "Anna the prophetess."

Let me say that I know of no person against whom there are more prejudices, nor anyone who more quickly disarms them. This strange faculty is the most powerful of her powers. She shoots a word like a sudden sunbeam through the thickest mist of people's doubts and accusations, and clears the sky in a moment. Questioned by some committee or delegation who have come to her with idle tales against her busy life, I have seen her swiftly gather together all the stones which they have cast, put them like the miner's quartz into the furnace, melt them with fierce and fervent heat, bring out of them the purest gold, stamp thereon her image and superscription as if she were sovereign of the realm, and then (as the marvel of it all) receive the sworn allegiance of the whole company on the spot. At one of her public meetings when the chair (as she hoped) would be occupied by Lucretia Mott, this venerable woman had been persuaded to decline this responsibility, but afterward stepped forward on the platform and lovingly kissed the young speaker in presence of the multitude. Her enemies (save those of her own household,) are strangers. To see her is to respect her—to know her is to vindicate her. She has some impetuous and headlong faults, but were she without the same traits which produce these she would not possess the mad and magnificent energies which (if she lives) will make her a heroine of history.

In conclusion, amid all the rush of her active life, she believes with Wordsworth that

"The gods approve the depth and not
The tumult of the soul."

So, whether buffeted by criticism or defamed by slander, she carries herself in that religious peace which, through all turbulence, is "a measureless content." When apparently about to be struck down, she gathers unseen strength and goes forward conquering and to conquer. Known only as a rash iconoclast, and ranked even with the most uncouth of those noise-makers who are waking a sleepy world before its time, she beats her daily gong of business and reform with notes not musical but strong, yet mellows the outward rudeness of the rhythm by the inward and devout song of one of the sincerest, most reverent, and divinely-gifted of human souls.

And The Truth Shall Make You Free: A Speech On The Principles Of Social Freedom

by Victoria C. Woodhull
First Female American Presidential Candidate

November 20, 1871

THE PRESENT CRISIS

When a deed is done for Freedom, through the broad
earth's aching breast
Runs a thrill of joy prophetic, trembling on from East to
West,
And the slave, where'er he cowers, feels the soul within
him climb
To the awful verge of manhood, as the energy sublime
Of a century bursts full-blossomed on the thorny stem of
Time.

Through the walls of hut and palace shoots the
instantaneous three
When the travail of the Ages wrings earth's systems to
and fro;
At the birth of each new Era, with a recognizing start,
Nation wildly at nation, standing with mute lips apart,
And glad Truth's yet mightier man-child leaps beneath
the Future's heart.

For mankind are one in spirit and an instinct bears along,

Round the earth's electric circle, the swift flash of right
and wrong;
Whether conscious or unconscious, yet Humanity's vast
frame
Through its ocean-sundered fibres feels the gush of joy or
shame;
In the gain or loss of race all the rest have equal claim.

Once to every man and nation comes the moment to
decide,
In the strife of Truth with Falsehood, for the good or evil
side;
Some great cause, God's new Messiah, offering each the
bloom or blight,
Parts the goats upon the lift hand and the sheep upon the
right,
And the choice goes by forever twixt that darkness and
the light.

Careless seems the great avenged; history's pages but
record
One death-grapple in the darkness twixt old systems and
the word;
Truth forever on the scaffold, Wrong forever on the
throne,-
Yet the scaffold sways the Future, and behind the dim
unknown,
Standeth God within the shadow, keeping waten above
his own.

We see dimly in the Present what is small and what is
great,

Slow of faith, how weak an arm turn the iron helm of
fate,
But the soul is still oracular; amid the market's din,
List the ominous stern whisper from the Debbie cave
within-
"They enclave their children's children who make
compromise with sin."

Then to side with Truth is noble, when we share her
wretched crust,
Ere her cause bring fame and profit, and tis prosperous to
be just;
When it is the above man chooses, while the coward
stands aside,
Doubting in his abject spirit, till his Lord is crucified,
And the multitude make virtue of the fifth they had
denied.

Count me o'er earth's chosen heroes-they were somle that
stood alone
While the men they agonized for hurled the
contumclioumtone
Stood serene, and down the future saw the golden beam
incline
To the side of perfect justice, mastered by their faith
divine,
By one man's plain truth to manhood and to God's
supreme design.

For Humanity sweeps onward; where to-day the martyr
stands,
On the morrow crouches Judas with the silver in his
hands;

Far in front the cross stands ready and the crackling fagots burn,
While the booting mob of yesterday in silent awe return
To glean up the scattered ashes into History's golden urn.

They have rights who dare maintain them; we are traitors to our sires,
Smothering in their holy ashes Freedom's new-lit altar fires:
Shall we make their creed our jailor? Shall we, in our haste to slay,
From the tombs of the old prophets steal the funeral lamps away
To light up the martyr-fagots round the prophets of to-day.

New occasions teach new duties; Time makes ancient good uncouth;
They must upward still, and onward, who would keep abreast of Truth;
So, before us gleam her camp-fires! we ourselves must Pilgrim be,
Launch our Mayflower, and steer boldly through the desperate winter sea,
Nor attempt the Future's portal with the Past's blood-rusted key.

December, 1845 .... James Russel Lowell

The Principles of Social Freedom

It has been said by a very wise person that there is a trinity in all things, the perfect unity of the trinity or a tri-unity being necessary to make a complete objective realization. Thus we have the theological Trinity: The Father, the Son and the Holy Ghost; or Cause, Effect and the Process of Evolution. Also the political Trinity: Freedom, Equality, Justice or Individuality, Unity, Adjustment; the first term of which is also resolvable into these parts, thus: Religious freedom, political freedom and social freedom, while Religion, Politics and Socialism are the Tri-unity of Humanity. There are also the beginning, the end and the intermediate space, time and motion, to all experiences of space, time and motion, and the diameter, circumference and area, or length, breadth and depth to all form.

Attention has been called to these scientific facts, for the purpose of showing that for any tri-unity to lack one of its terms is for it to be incomplete; and that in the order of natural evolution, if two terms exist, the third must also exist.

Religious freedom does, in a measure, exist in this country, but not yet perfectly; that is to say, a person is not entirely independent of public opinion regarding matters of conscience. Though since Political freedom has existed in theory, every person has the right to entertain any religious theory he or she may conceive to be true, and government can take no cognizance thereof-he is only amenable to society -despotism. The necessary corollary to Religious and Political freedom is Social freedom, which is the third term of the trinity; that is to say, if Religious and Political freedom exist, perfected, Social freedom is at that very moment guaranteed, since Social freedom is the fruit of that condition.

We find the principle of Individual freedom was quite dormant until it began to speak against the right of religious despots, to determine what views should be advocated regarding the relations of the creature to the Creator. Persons began to find ideas creeping into their souls at variance with the teachings of the clergy; which ideas became so strongly fixed that they were compelled to protest against Religious Despotism. Thus, in the sixteenth century, was begun the battle for Individual freedom. The claim that rulers had no right to control the consciences of the people was boldly made, and right nobly did the fight continue until the absolute right to individual opinion was wrung from the despots, and even the common people found themselves entitled to not only entertain but also to promulgate any belief or theory of which they could conceive.

With yielding the control over the consciences of individuals, the despots had no thought of giving up any right to their persons. But Religious freedom naturally led the people to question the right of this control, and in the eighteenth century a new protest found expression in the French Revolution, and it was baptized by a deluge of blood yielded by thousands of lives. But not until an enlightened people freed themselves from English tyranny was the right to self-government acknowledged in theory, and not yet even is it fully accorded in practice, as a legitimate result of that theory.

It may seem to be a strange proposition to make, that there is no such thing yet existent in the world as self-government, in its political aspects. But such is the fact. If self-government be the rule, every self must be its subject. If a person govern, not only himself but others, that is despotic government, and it matters not if that control be over one or over a thousand individuals, or over a nation; in each case it, would be the same principle of power exerted outside of self and over others, and this is despotism, whether it is exercised by one person over his subjects, or by twenty persons over a nation, or by one-half the people of a nation over the other half thereof. There is no escaping the fact that the principle by which the male citizens of these United States assume to rule the female citizens is not that of self-government, but that of despotism; and so the fact is that poets have sung songs of freedom, and anthems of liberty have resounded for an empty shadow.

King George III, and his Parliament denied our forefathers the right to make their own laws; they rebelled, and being successful, inaugurated this government. But men do not seem to comprehend that they are now pursuing toward women the same despotic course that King George pursued toward the American colonies.

But what is freedom? The press and our male governors are very much exercised about this question, since a certain set of resolutions were launched upon the public by Paulina Wright Davis at Apollo Hall, May 12, 1871. They are as follows:

> Resolved, That the basis of order is freedom from bondage; not, indeed, of such "order" as resigned in Warsaw, which grew out of the bondage; but of such order as reigns in Heaven, which grows out of that developed manhood and womanhood in which each becomes "a law unto himself."

> Resolved, That freedom is a principle, and that as such it may be trusted to ultimate in harmonious social results, as in America, it has resulted in harmonious and beneficent political results; that it has not hitherto been adequately trusted in the social domain, and that the woman's movement means no less than the complete social as well as the political enfranchisement of mankind.

> Resolved, That the evils, sufferings and disabilities of women, as well as of men, are social still more than they are political, and that a statement of woman's rights which ignores the rights of self-ownership as the first of all rights is insufficient to meet the demand, and is ceasing to enlist the enthusiasm and even the common interest of the most intelligent portion of the community.

> Resolved, That the principle of freedom is one principle, and not a collection of many different and unrelated principles; that there is not at bottom one principle of freedom of conscience as in Protestantism, and another principle of freedom from slavery as in Abolitionism, another of freedom of locomotion as in our dispensing in America with the

passport system of Europe, another of the freedom of the press as in Great Britain and America, and still another of social freedom at large; but that freedom is on and indivisible; and that slavery is so also; that freedom and bondage or restriction is the alternative and the issue, alike, in every case; and that if freedom is good in one case it is good in all; that we in America have builded on freedom, politically, and that we cannot consistently recoil from that expansion of freedom which shall make it the basis of all our institutions; and finally, that so far as we have trusted it, it has proved, in the main, safe and profitable.

Now, is there anything so terrible in the language of these resolutions as to threaten the foundations of society? They assert that every individual has a better right to herself or himself than any other person can have. No living soul, who does not desire to have control over, or ownership in, another person, can have any valid objection to anything expressed in these resolutions. Those who are not willing to give up control over others; who desire to own somebody beside themselves; who are constitutionally predisposed against self-government and the giving of the same freedom to others that they demand for themselves, will of course object to them, and such are the people with whom we shall have to contend in this new struggle for a greater liberty

Now, the individual is either self-owned and self-possessed or is not so self-possessed. If he be self-owned, he is so because he has an inherent right to self, which right cannot be delegated to any second person; a right-as the American Declaration of Independence has it-which is "inalienable." The individual must be responsible to self and God for his acts. If he be owned and possessed by some second person, then there is no such thing as individuality: and that for which the world has been striving these thousands of years is the merest myth.

But against this irrational, illogical, inconsequent and irreverent theory I boldly oppose the spirit of the age-that spirit which will not admit all civilization to be a failure, and all past experience to count for nothing; against that demagogism, I oppose the plain principle of freedom in its fullest, purest, broadest, deepest application and significance-the freedom which we see exemplified in the starry firmament, where whirl innumerable worlds, and never one of which is made to lose its individuality, but each performs its part in the grand economy of the universe, giving and receiving its natural repulsions and attractions; we also see it exemplified in every department of nature about us: in the sunbeam and the dewdrop; in the storm-cloud and the spring shower; in the driving snow and the congealing rain-all of which speak more eloquently than can human tongue of the heavenly beauty, symmetry and purity of the spirit of freedom which in them reigns untrammeled.

Our government is based upon the proposition that: All men and women are born free and equal and entitled to certain inalienable rights, among which are life, liberty and the pursuit of happiness. Now what we, who demand social freedom, ask, is simply that the government of this country shall be administered in accordance with the spirit of this proposition. Nothing more, nothing less. If that proposition mean anything, it means just what it says, without qualification, limitation or equivocation. It means that every person who comes into the world of outward existence is of equal right as an individual, and is free as an individual, and that he or she is entitled to pursue happiness in whatever direction he or she may choose. Now this is absolutely true of all men and all women. But just here the wise-acres stop and tell us that everybody must not pursue happiness in his or her own way; since to do so absolutely, would be to have no protection against the action of individual. These good and well-meaning people only see one-half of what is involved in the proposition. They look at a single individual and for the time lose sight of all others. They do not take into their consideration that every other individual beside the one whom they contemplate is equally with him entitled to the same freedom; and that each is free within the area of his or her individual sphere; and not free within the sphere of any other individual whatever. They do not seem to recognize the fact that the moment one person gets out of his sphere into the sphere of another, that other must protect him or herself against such invasion of rights. They do not seem to be able to comprehend that the moment one person encroaches upon another person's rights he or she ceases to be a free man or woman and becomes a despot. To all such persons we assert: that it is freedom and not despotism which we advocate and demand; and we will as rigorously demand that individuals be restricted to their freedom as any person dare to demand; and as rigorously demand that people who are predisposed to be tyrants instead of free men or women shall, by the government, be so restrained as to make the exercise of their proclivities impossible.

If life, liberty and the pursuit of happiness are inalienable rights in the individual, and government is based upon that inalienability, then it must follow as a legitimate sequence that the functions of that government are to guard and protect the right to life, liberty and the pursuit of happiness, to the end that every person may have the most perfect exercise of them. And the most perfect exercise of such rights is only attained when every individual is not only fully protected in his rights, but also strictly restrained to the exercise of them within his own sphere, and positively prevented from proceeding beyond its limits, so as to encroach upon the sphere of another: unless that other first agree thereto.

From these generalizations certain specializations are deducible, by which all questions of rights must be determined:

1. Every living person has certain rights of which no law can rightfully deprive him.

2. Aggregates of persons form communities, who erect governments to secure regularity and order.

3. Order and harmony can alone be secured in a community where every individual of whom it is composed is fully protected in the exercise of all individual rights.

4. Any government which enacts laws to deprive

individuals of the free exercise of their right to life, liberty and the pursuit of happiness is despotic, and such laws are not binding upon the people who protest against them, whether they be a majority or a minority.

5. When every individual is secure in the possession and exercise of all his rights, then everyone is also secure from the interference of all other parties.

6. All inharmony and disorder arise from the attempts of individuals to interfere with the rights of other individuals, or from the protests of individuals against governments for depriving them of their inalienable rights.

These propositions are all self-evident, and must be accepted by every person who subscribes to our theory of government, based upon the sovereignty of the individual; consequently any law in force which conflicts with any of them is not in accord with that theory and is therefore unconstitutional.

A fatal error into which most people fall, is, that rights are conceded to governments, while they are only possessed of the right to perform duties, as a farther analysis will show:

In the absence of any arrangement by the members of a community to secure order, each individual is a law unto himself, so far as he is capable of maintaining it against all other individuals; but at the mercy of all such who are bent on conquest. Such a condition is anarchy.

But if in individual freedom the whole number of individuals unite to secure equality and protection to themselves, they thereby surrender no individual rights to the community, but they simply invest the community with the power to perform certain specified duties, which are set forth in the law of their combination. Hence a government erected by the people is invested, not with the rights of the people, but with the duty of protecting and maintaining their rights intact; and any government is a failure or a success just so far as it fails or succeeds in this duty; and these are the legitimate functions of government.

I have before said that every person has the right to, and can, determine for himself what he will do, even to taking the life of another. But it is equally true that the attacked person has the right to defend his life against such assault. If the person succeed in taking the life, he thereby demonstrates that he is a tyrant who is at all times liable to invade the right to life, and that every individual of the community is put in jeopardy by the freedom of this person. Hence it is the duty of the government to so restrict the freedom of this person as to make it impossible for him to ever again practice such tyranny. Here the duty of the community ceases. It has no right to take the life of the individual. That is his own, inalienably vested in him, both by God and the Constitution.

A person may also appropriate the property of another if he so choose, and there is no way to prevent it; but once having thus invaded the rights of another, the whole community is in danger from the propensity of this person. It is therefore the duty of government to so restrain the liberty of the person as to prevent him from invading the spheres of other persons in a manner against which he himself demands, and is entitled to, protection.

The same rule applies to that class of persons who have a propensity to steal or to destroy the character of others. This class of encroachers upon others' rights, in some senses, are more reprehensible than any other, save only those who invade the rights of life; since for persons to be made to appear what they are not may, perhaps, be to place them in such relations with third persons as to destroy their means of pursuing happiness. Those who thus invade the pursuit of happiness by others, should be held to be the worst enemies of society; proportionably worse than the common burglar or thief, as what they destroy is more valuable than is that which the burglar or thief can appropriate. For robbery there may be some excuse, since what is stolen may be required to contribute to actual needs; but that which the assassin of character appropriates does neither good to himself nor to anyone else, and makes the loser poor indeed. Such persons are the worst enemies of society.

I have been thus explicit in the analysis of the principles of freedom in their application to the common affairs of life, because I desired, before approaching the main subject, to have it well settled as to what may justly be considered the rights of individuals; or in other words what individual sovereignty implies.

It would be considered a very unjust and arbitrary, as

well as an unwise thing, if the government of the United States were to pass a law compelling persons to adhere during life to everything they should to-day accept as their religion, their politics and their vocations. It would manifestly be a departure from the true functions of government. The apology for what I claim to be an invasion of the rights of the individual is found in the law to enforce contracts. While the enforcement of contracts in which pecuniary considerations are involved is a matter distinct and different from that of the enforcement of contracts involving the happiness of individuals, even in them the governments has no legitimate right to interfere. The logical deduction of the right of two people to make a contract without consulting the government, or any third party, is the right of either or both of the parties to withdraw without consulting any third party, either in reference to its enforcement or as to damages.

As has been stated, such an arrangement is the result of the exercise of the right of two or more individuals to unite their rights, perfectly independent of every outside party. There is neither right nor duty beyond the uniting-the contracting-individuals. So neither can there be an appeal to a third party to settle any difference which may arise between such parties. All such contracts have their legitimate basis and security in the honor and purposes of the contracting parties. It seems to me that, admitting our theory of government, no proposition can be plainer than is this, notwithstanding the practice is entirely different. But I am now discussing the abstract principles of the rights of freedom, which no practice that may be in vogue must be permitted to deter us from following to legitimate conclusions.

In all general contracts, people have the protection of government in contracting for an hour, a day, a week, a year, a decade, or a life, and neither the government nor any other third party or persons, or aggregates of persons ever think of making a scale of respectability, graduated by the length of time for which the contracts are made and maintained. Least of all does the government require that any of these contracts shall be entered into for life. Why should the social relations of the sexes be made subject to a different theory? All enacted laws that are for the purpose of perpetuating conditions which are themselves the results of evolution are so many obstructions in the path of progress; since if an effect attained to-day is made the ultimate, progress stops. "Thus far shalt thou go, and no farther," is not the adage of a progressive age like the present. Besides, there can be no general law made to determine what individual cases demand, since a variety of conditions cannot be subject to one and the same rule of operation. Here we arrive at the most important of all facts relating to human needs and experiences: That while every human being has a distinct individuality, and is entitled to all the rights of a sovereign over it, it is not taken into the consideration that no two of these individualities are made up of the self-same powers and experiences, and therefore cannot be governed by the same law to the same purposes.

I would recall the attention of all objecting egotists, Pharisees and would-be regulators of society to the true functions of government-to protect the complete exercise of individual rights, and what they are no living soul except the individual has any business to determine or to meddle with, in any way whatever, unless his own rights are first infringed.

If a person believe that a certain theory is a truth, and consequently the right thing to advocate and practice, but from its being unpopular or against established public opinion does not have the moral courage to advocate or practice it, that person is a moral coward and traitor to his own conscience, which God gave for a guide and guard.

What I believe to be the truth I endeavor to practice, and, in advocating it, permit me to say I shall speak so plainly that none may complain that I did not make myself understood.

The world has come up to the present time through the outworking of religious, political, philosophical and scientific principles, and today we stand upon the threshold of greater in more important things than have ever interested the intellect of man. We have arrived where the very foundation of all that has been must be analyzed and understood-and this foundation is the relation of the sexes. These are the bases of society-the very last to secure attention, because the most comprehensive of subjects.

All other departments of inquiry which have their fountain in society have been formulated into special sciences, and made legitimate and popular subjects for investigation, but the science of society itself has been, and still is, held to be too sacred a thing for science to lay its rude hands upon. But of the relations of science to society we may say the same that has been said of the relations of science to religion: "That religion has always wanted to do good, and now science is going to tell it how to do it."

Over the sexual relations, marriages have endeavored to preserve sway and to hold the people in subjection to what has been considered a standard of moral purity. Whether this has been successful or not may be determined from the fact that there are scores of thousands of women who are denominated prostitutes, and who are supported by hundreds of thousands of men who should, for like reasons, also be denominated prostitutes, since what will change a woman into a prostitute must also necessarily change a man into the same.

This condition, called prostitution, seems to be the great evil at which religion and public morality hurl their special weapons of condemnation, as the sum total of all diabolism; since for a woman to be a prostitute is to deny her not only all Christian, but also all humanitarian rights.

But let us inquire into this matter, to see just what it is; not in the vulgar or popular, or even legal sense, but in a purely scientific and truly moral sense.

It must be remembered that we are seeking after such for the sake of the truth, and in utter disregard of everything except the truth; that is to say, we are seeking for the truth, "let it be what it may and lead where it may." To illustrate, I would say the extremist thing possible. If blank materialism were true, it would be best for the world to know it.

If there be any who are not in harmony with this desire, then such have nothing to do with what I have to say, for it will be said regardless of antiquate forms or fossilized dogmas, but in the simplest and least offending language that I can choose.

If there is anything in the whole universe that should enlist the earnest attention of everybody, and their support and advocacy to secure it, it is that upon which the true Welfare and happiness of everybody depends. Now to what more than to anything else do humanity owe their welfare and happiness? Most clearly to being born into earthly existence with a sound and perfect physical, mental and moral beginning of life, with no taint or disease attaching to them, either mentally, morally or physically. To be so born involves the harmony of conditions which will produce such results. To have such conditions involves the existence of such relations of the sexes as will in themselves produce them.

Now I will put the question direct. Are not these eminently proper subjects for inquiry and discussion, not in that manner of maudlin sentimentality in which it has been the habit, but in a dignified, open, lowest and fearless way, in which subjects of so great importance should be inquired into and discussed?

An exhaustive treatment of these subjects would involve

the inquiry what should be the chief end to be gained by entering into sexual relations. This I must simply answer by saying, "Good children, who will not need to regenerated," and pass to the consideration of the relations themselves.

All the relations between the sexes that are recognized as legitimate are denominated marriage. But of what does marriage consist? This very pertinent question requires settlement before any real progress can be made as to what Social Freedom and Prostitution mean. It is admitted by everybody that marriage is a union of the opposite in sex, but is it a principle of nature outside of all law, or is it a law outside of all nature? Where is the point before reaching which it is not marriage, but having reached which it is marriage? Is it where two meet and realize that the love clements of their nature are harmonious, and that they blend into and make one purpose of life? or is it where a soulless form is pronounced over two who know no commingling of life's hopes?

Or are both these processes required-first, the marriage union without the law, to be afterward solemnized by the law? If both terms are required, does the marriage continue after the first departs? or if the restrictions of the law are removed and the love continues, does marriage continue? or if the law unite two who hate each other, is that marriage? Thus are presented all the possible aspects of the case.

The courts hold if the law solemnly pronounce two married, that they are married, whether love is present or not. But this really such a marriage as this enlightened age should demand? No! It is a stupidly arbitrary law, which can find no analogies in nature. Nature proclaims in broadest terms, and all her subjects re-echo the same grand truth, that sexual unions, which result in reproduction, are marriage. And sex exists wherever there is reproduction.

By analogy, the same law ascends into the sphere of and applies among men and women; for are not they a part and parcel of nature in which this law exists as a principle? This law of nature by which men and women are united by love is God's marriage law, the enactments of men to the contrary notwithstanding. And the precise results of this marriage will be determined by the character of those united; all the experiences evolved from the marriage being the legitimate sequences thereof.

marriage must consist either of love or of law, since it may exist in form with either term absent; that is to say, people may be married by law and all love be lacking; and they may also be married by love and lack all sanction of law. True marriage must in reality consist entirely either of law or love, since there can be no compromise between the law of nature and statute law by which the former shall yield to the latter.

Law cannot change what nature has already determined. Neither will love obey if law command. Law cannot compel two to love. It has nothing to do either with love or with its absence. Love is superior to all law, and so also is hate, indifference, disgust and all other human sentiments which are evoked in the relations of the sexes.

It legitimately and logically follows, if love have anything to do with marriage, that law has nothing to do with it. And on the contrary, if law have anything to do with marriage, that love has nothing to do with it. And there is no escaping the deduction. If the test of the rights of the individual be applied to determine which of these propositions is the true one, what will be the result?

Two persons, a male and a female, meet, and are drawn together by a mutual attraction-a natural feeling unconsciously arising within their natures of which neither has any control-which is denominated love. This a matter that concerns these two, and no other living soul has any human right to say aye, yes or no, since it is a matter in which none except the two have any right to be involved, and from which it is the duty of these two to exclude every other person, since no one can love for another or determine why another loves.

If true, mutual, natural attraction be sufficiently strong to be the dominant power, them it decides marriage; and if it be so decided, no law which may be in force can any more prevent the union than a human law could prevent the transformation of water into vapor, or the confluence of two streams; and for precisely the same reasons: that it is a natural law which is obeyed; which law is as high above human law as perfection is high above imperfection. They marry and obey this higher law than man can make-a law as old as the universe and as immortal as the elements, and for which there is no substitute.

They are sexually united, to be which is to be married by

nature, and to be thus married is to be united by God. This marriage is performed without special mental volition upon the part of either, although the intellect may approve what the affections determine; thus is to say, they marry because they love, and they love because they can neither prevent nor assist it. Suppose after this marriage has continued an indefinite time, the unity between them departs, could they any more prevent it than they can prevent the love? It came without their bidding, may it not also go without their bidding? And if it go, does not the marriage cease, and should any third persons or parties, either as individuals or government, attempt to compel the continuance of a unity wherein none of the elements of the union remain?

At no point in the process designated has there been any other than an exercise of the right of the two individuals to pursue happiness in their own way, which may has neither crossed nor interfered with anyone else's right to the same pursuit; therefore, there is no call for a law to change, modify, protect or punish this exercise. It must be concluded, then, if individuals have the Constitutional right to pursue happiness in their own way, that all compelling laws of marriage and divorce are despotic, being remnants of the barbaric ages in which they were originated, and utterly unfitted for an age so advanced upon that, and so enlightened in the general principles of freedom and equality, as is this.

It must be remembered that it is the sphere of government to perform the duties which are required of it by the people, and that it has, in itself, no rights to exercise. These belong exclusively to the people whom it represents. It is one of the rights of a citizen to have a voice in determining what the duties of government shall be, and also provide how that right may be exercised; but government should not prohibit any right.

To love is a right higher than Constitutions or laws. It is a right which Constitutions and laws can neither give nor take, and with which they have nothing whatever to do, since in its very nature it is forever independent of both Constitutions and laws, and exists-comes and goes-in spite of them. Governments might just as well assume to determine how people shall exercise their right to think or to say that they shall not think at all, as to assume to determine that they shall not love, or how they may love, or that they shall love.

The proper sphere of government in regard to the relations of the saxes, is to enact such laws as in the present conditions of society are necessary to protect each individual in the free exercise of his or her right to love, and also to protect each individual from the forced interference of every other person, that would compel him or her to submit to any action which is against their wish and will. If the law do this it fulfills its duty. If the law do not afford this protection, and worse still, if it sanction this interference with the rights of an individual, then it is infamous law and worthy only of the old-time despotism; since individual tyranny forms no part of the guarantee of, or the right to, individual freedom.

It is therefore a strictly legitimate conclusion that where there is no love as a basis of marriage there should be no marriage, and if that which was the basis of a marriage is taken away that the marriage also ceases from the time, statute laws to the contrary notwithstanding.

Such is the character of the law that permeates nature from simplest organic forms-units of nucleated protoplasm to the most complex aggregation thereof-the human form. Having determined that marriage consists of a union resulting from love, without any regard whatever to the sanction of law, and consequently that the sexual relations resulting therefrom are strictly legitimate and natural, it is a very simple matter to determine what part of the sexual relations which are maintained are prostitutions of the relations.

It is certain by this Higher Law, that marriages of convenience, and, still more, marriages characterized by mutual or partial repugnance, are adulterous. And it does not matter whether the repugnance arises before or subsequently to the marriage ceremony. Compulsion, whether of the law or of a false public opinion, is detestable, as an element even, in the regulation of the most tender and important of all human relations.

I do not care where it is that sexual commerce results from the dominant power of one sex over the other, compelling him or her to submission against the instincts of love, and where hate or disgust is present, whether it be in the gilded palaces of Fifth avenue or in the lowest purlieus of Greene street, there is prostitution, and all the law that a thousand State Assemblies may pass cannot make it otherwise.

I know whereof I speak; I have seen the most damning

misery resulting from legalized prostitution. Misery such as the most degraded of those against whom society has shut her doors never know. Thousands of poor, weak, unresisting wives are yearly murdered, who stand in spirit-life looking down upon the sickly, half made-up children left behind, imploring humanity for the sake of honor and virtue to look into this matter, to look into it to the very bottom, and bring out into the fair daylight all the blackened, sickening deformities that have so long been hidden by the screen of public opinion and a sham morality.

It does not matter how much it may still be attempted to gloss these things over and to label them sound and pure; you, each and every one of you, know that what I say is truth, and if you question your own souls you dare not reply: it is not so. If these things to which I refer, but of which I shudder to think, are not abuses of the sexual relations, what are?

You may or may not think there is help for them, but I say Heaven help us if such barbarism cannot be cured.

I would not be understood to say that there are no good conditions in the present marriage state. By no means do I say this; on the contrary, a very large proportion of present social relations are commendable-are as good as the present status of society makes possible. But what I do assert, and, that most positively, is, that all which is good and commendable, now existing, would continue to exist if all marriage laws were repealed to-morrow. Do you not perceive that law has nothing to do in continuing the relations which are based upon continuous love?

These are not results of the law to which, perhaps, their subjects yielded a willing or unwilling obedience. Such relations exist in spite of the law; would have existed had there been no law, and would continue to exist were the law annulled.

It is not of the good there is in the present condition of marriage that I complain, but of the ill, nearly the whole of which is the direct result of the law which continues the relations in which it exists. It seems to be the general argument that if the law of marriage were annulled it would follow that everybody must necessarily separate, and that all present family relations would be sundered, and complete anarchy result therefrom. Now, whoever makes that argument either does so thoughtlessly or else he is dishonest; since if he make it after having given any consideration thereto, he must know it to be false. And if he have given it no consideration then is he no proper judge. I give it as my opinion, founded upon an extensive knowledge of, and intimate acquaintance with, married people, if marriage laws were repealed that less than a fourth of those now married would immediately separate, and that one-half of these would return to their allegiance voluntarily within one year; only those who, under every consideration of virtue and good, should be separate, would permanently remain separated. And objectors as well as I know it would be so. I assert that it is false to assume that chaos would result from the abrogation of marriage laws, and on the contrary affirm that from that very hour the chaos was existing would begin to turn into order and harmony. What then creates social disorder? Very clearly, the attempt to exercise powers over human rights which are not warrantable upon the hypothesis of the existence of human rights which are inalienable in, and sacred to, the individual.

It is true there is no enacted law compelling people to marry, and it is therefore argued that if they do marry they should always be compelled to abide thereby. But there is a law higher than any human enactments which does compel marriage-the law of nature-the law of God. There being this law in the constitution of humanity, which, operating freely, guarantees marriage, why should men enforce arbitrary rules and forms? These, though having no virtue in themselves, if not complied with by men and women, they in the meantime obeying the law of their nature, bring down upon them the condemnations of an interfering community. Should people, then, voluntarily entering legal marriage be held thereby "till death do them part?" Most emphatically no, if the desire to do so do not remain. How can people who enter upon marriage in utter ignorance of that which is to render the union happy or miserable be able to say that they will always "love and live together." They may take these vows upon them in perfect good faith and repent of them in sackcloth and ashes within a twelve-month.

I think it will be generally conceded that without love there should be no marriage. In the constitution of things nothing can be more certain. This basic fact is fatal to the theory of marriage for life: since if love is what determines marriage, so, also, should it determine its continuance. If it be primarily right of men and women to take on the marriage relation of their own free will and accord, so, too, does it remain their right to determine how long it shall continue and when it shall cease. But to be respectable (?) people must comply with the law, and thousands do comply therewith, while in their hearts they protest against it as an unwarrantable interference and proscription of their rights. Marriage laws that would be consistent with the theory of individual rights would be such as would regulate these relations, such as regulate all other associations of people. They should only be obliged to file marriage articles, containing whatever provisions may be agreed upon, as to their personal rights, rights of property, of children, or whatever else they may deem proper for them to agree upon. And whatever these articles might be, they should in all cases be equally entitled to public respect and protection. Should separation afterward come, nothing more should be required than the simple filing of counter articles.

There are hundreds of lawyers who subsist by inventing schemes by which people may obtain divorces, and the people desiring divorces resort to all sorts of tricks and crimes to get them. And all this exists because there are laws which would compel the oneness of those to whom unity is beyond the realm of possibility. There are another class of persons who, while virtually divorced, endeavor to maintain a respectable position in society, by agreeing to disagree, each following his and her individual ways, behind the cloak of legal marriage. Thus there are hundreds of men and women who to external appearances are husband and wife, but in reality are husband or wife to quite different persons.

If the conditions of society were completely analyzed, it would be found that all persons whom the law holds married against their wishes find some way to evade the law and to live the life they desire. Of what use, then, is the law except to make hypocrites and pretenders of a sham respectability?

But, exclaims a very fastidious person, then you would have all women become prostitutes! By no means would I have any woman become a prostitute. But if by nature women are so, all the virtue they possess being of the legal kind, and not that which should exist with or without law, then I say they will not become prostitutes because the law is repealed, since at heart they are already so. If there is no virtue, no honesty, no purity, no trust among women except as created by the law, I say heaven help our morality, for nothing human can help it.

It seems to me that no grosser insult could be offered to woman than to insinuate that she is honest and virtuous only because the law compels her to be so; and little do men and women realize the obloquy thus cast upon society, and still less do women realize what they admit of their sex by such assertions. I honor and worship that purity which exists in the soul of every noble man or woman, while I pity the woman who is virtuous simply because a law compels her.

But, says another objector, though the repeal of marriage laws might operate well enough in all those cases where a mutual love or hate would determine continuous marriage or immediate divorce, how can a third class of cases be justified, in which but one of the parties desire the separation, while the other clings to the unity?

70

I assume, in the first place, when there is not mutual love there is no union to continue and nothing to justify, and it has already been determined that, as marriage should have love as a basis, if love depart marriage also departs. But laying this aside, see if there can any real good or happiness possibly result from an enforced continuance of marriage upon the part of one party thereto. Let all persons take this question home to their own souls, and there determine if they could find happiness in holding unwilling hearts in bondage. It is against the nature of things that any satisfaction can result from such a state of things except it be the satisfaction of knowing that you have succeeded in virtually imprisoning the person whom you profess to love, and that would be demoniacal.

Again. It must be remembered that the individual affairs of two persons are not the subject of interference by any third party, and if one of them chose to separate, there is no power outside of the two which can rightly interfere to prevent. Beside, who is to determine whether there will be more happiness sacrificed by a continuation or a separation. If a person is fully determined to separate, it is proof positive that another feeling stronger than all his or her sentiments of duty determine it. And here, again, who but the individual is to determine which course will secure the most good? Suppose that a separation is desired because one of the two loves and is loved elsewhere. In this case, if the union be maintained by force, at least two of three, and, probably, all three persons will be made unhappy thereby; whereas if separation come and the other union be consummated, there will be but one, unhappy. So even here, if the greatest good of the greatest number is to rule, separation is not only legitimate, but desirable. In all other things except marriage it is always held to be the right thing to do to break a bad bargain or promise just as soon as possible, and I hold that of all things in which this rule should apply, it should first apply to marriages.

Now, let me ask, would it not rather be the Christian way, in such cases, to say to the disaffected party: "Since you no longer love me, go your way and be happy, and make those to whom you go happy also." I know of no higher, holier love than that described, and of no more beautiful expression of it than was given in the columns of the Woman's Journal, of Boston, whose conductors have felt called upon to endeavor to convince the people that it has no affiliation with those who hold to no more radical doctrine of Free Love than they proclaim as follows:

> "The love that I cannot command is not mine; let me not disturb myself about it, nor attempt to filch it from its rightful owner. A heart that I supposed mine has drifted and gone. Shall I go in pursuit? Shall I forcibly capture the truant and transfix it with the barb of my selfish affections, pin it to the wall of my chamber? God forbid! Rather let me leave my doors and windows open, intent only on living so nobly that the best cannot fail to be drawn to me by an irresistible attraction."

To me it is impossible to frame words into sentences more holy, pure and true than are these. I would ever carry them in my soul as my guide and guard, feeling that in living by them happiness would certainly be mine. To the loving wife who mourns a lost heart, let me recommend them as a panacea. To the loving husband whose soul is desolate, let me offer these as words of healing balm. They will live in history, to make their writer the loved and revered of unborn generations.

The tenth commandment of the Decalogue says: "Thou shalt not covet thy neighbor's wife." And Jesus, in the beautiful parable of the Samaritan who fell among thieves, asks: "Who is thy neighbor?" and answers his own question in a way to lift the conception wholly out of the category of mere local proximity into a sublime spiritual conception. In other words, he spiritualizes the word and sublimates the morality of the commandment. In the same spirit I ask now, Who is a wife? And I answer, not the woman who, ignorant of her own feelings, or with lying lips, has promised, in hollow ceremonial, and before the law, to love, but she who really loves most, and most truly, the man who commands her affections, and who in turn loves her, with or without the ceremony of marriage; and the man who holds the heart of such a woman in such a relation is "thy neighbor," and that woman is "thy neighbor's wife" meant in the commandment; and whosoever, though he should have been a hundred times married to her by the law, shall claim, or covet even, the possession of that woman as against her true lover and husband in the spirit, sins against the commandment.

We know positively that Jesus would have answered in that way. He has defined for us "the neighbor," not in the paltry and commonplace sense, but spiritually. He has

73

said. "He that looketh on a woman to lust after her hath committed adultery with her already in his heart." So, therefore, he spiritualized the idea of adultery. In the kingdom of heaven, to be prayed for daily, to come on earth, there is to be no "marrying or giving in marriage," that is to say, formally and legally; but spiritual marriage must always exist, and had Jesus been called on to define a wife, can anybody doubt that he would, in the same spirit, the spiritualizing tendency and character of all his doctrine, have spiritualized the marriage relation as absolutely as he did the breach of it? that he would, in other words, have said in meaning precisely what I now say? And when Christian ministers are no longer afraid or ashamed to be Christians they will embrace this doctrine. Free Love will be an integral part of the religion of the future.

It can now be asked: What is the legitimate sequence of Social Freedom? To which I unhesitatingly reply: Free Love, or freedom of the affections. "And are you a Free Lover? is the almost incredulous query.

I repeat a frequent reply: "I am; and I can honestly, in the fullness of my soul, raise on my voice to my Marker, and thank Him that I am, and that I have had the strength and the devotion to truth to stand before this traducing and vilifying community in a manner representative of that which shall come with healing on its wings for the bruised hearts and crushed affections of humanity."

And to those who denounce me for this I reply: "Yes, I am a Free Lover. I have an inalienable, constitutional and natural right to love whom I may, to love as long or as short a period as I can; to change that love every day if I please, and with that right neither you nor any law you can frame have any right to interfere. And I have the further right to demand a free and unrestricted exercise of that right, and it is your duty not only to accord it, but, as a community, to see that I am protected in it. I trust that I am fully understood, for I mean just that, and nothing less!

To speak thus plainly and pointedly is a duty I owe to myself. The press have stigmatized me to the world as an advocate, theoretically and practically, of the doctrine of Free Love, upon which they have placed their stamp of moral deformity; the vulgar and inconsequent definition which they hold makes the theory an abomination. And though this conclusion is a no more legitimate and reasonable one than that would be which should call the Golden Rule a general license to all sorts of debauch, since Free Love bears the same relations to the moral deformities of which it stands accused as does the Golden Rule to the Law of the Despot, yet it obtains among many intelligent people. But they claim, in the language of one of these exponents, that "Words belong to the people; they are the common property of the mob. Now the common use, among the mob, of the term Free Love, is a synonym for promiscuity." Against this absurd proposition I oppose the assertion that words do not belong to the mob, but to that which they represent. Words are the exponents and interpretations of ideas. If I use a word which exactly interprets and represents what I would be understood to mean, shall I go to the mob and ask of them what interpretation they choose to place upon it? If lexicographers, when they prepare their dictionaries, were to go to the mob for the rendition of words, what kind of language would we have?

I claim that freedom means to be free, let the mob claim to the contrary as strenuously as they may. And I claim that love means an exhibition of the affections, let the mob claim what they may. And therefore, in compounding these words into Free Love, I claim that united they mean, and should be used to convey, their united definitions, the mob to the contrary notwithstanding. And when the term Free Love finds a place in dictionaries, it will prove my claim to have been correct, and that the mob have not received the attention of the lexicographers, since it will not be set down to signify sexual debauchery, and that only, or in any governing sense.

It is not only usual but also just, when people adopt a new theory, or promulgate a new doctrine, that they give it a name significant of its character. There are, however, exceptional cases to be found in all ages. The Jews coined the name of Christians, and, with withering contempt, hurled it upon the early followers of Christ. It was the most opprobrious epithet they could invent to express their detestation of those humble but honest and brave people. That name has now come to be considered as a synonym of all that is good, true and beautiful in the highest departments of our natures, and in revered in all civilized nations.

In precisely the same manner the Pharisees of to-day, who hold themselves to be representative of all there is that is good ad pure, as did the Pharisees of old, have coined the word Free-Love, and flung it upon all who believe not alone in Religious and Political Freedom, but in that larger Freedom, which includes both these, Social Freedom.

For my part, I am extremely obliged to our thoughtful Pharisaical neighbors for the kindness shown us in the invention of so appropriate a name. If there is a more beautiful word in the English language than love, that word is freedom, and that these two words, which, with us, attach or belong to everything that is pure and good, should have been joined by our enemies, and handed over to us already coined, is certainly a high consideration, for which we should never cease to be thankful. And when we shall be accused of all sorts of wickedness and vileness by our enemies, who in this have been so just, may I not hope that, remembering how much they have done for us, we may be able to say, "Father, forgive them, for they know not what they do," and to forgive them ourselves with or whole hearts.

Of the love that says: "Bless me, darling;" of the love so called, which is nothing but selfishness, the appropriation of another soul as the means of one's own happiness merely, there is abundance in the world; and the still more animal, the mere desire for temporary gratification, with little worthy the name of love, also abounds. Even these are best left free, since as evils they will thus be best cured; but of that celestial love which say: "Bless you, darling," and which strives continually to confer blessing; of that genuine love whose office it is to bless others or another, there cannot be too much in the world, and when it shall be fully understood that this is the love which we mean and commend there will be no objection to the term Free Love, and none to the thing signified.

We not only accept our name, but we contend that none other could so well signify the real character of that which it designates-to be free and to love. But our enemies must be reminded that the fact of the existence and advocacy of such a doctrine cannot immediately elevate to high condition the great number who have been kept in degradation and misery by previous false systems. They must not expect at this early day of the new doctrine, that all debauchery has been cleaned out of men and women. In the haunts where it retreats, the benign influence of its magic presence has not yet penetrated. They must not expect that brutish men and debased women have as yet been touched by its wand of hope, and that they have already obeyed the bidding to come up higher. They must not expect that ignorance and fleshly lust have already been lifted to the region of intellect and moral purity. They must not expect that Free Love, before it is more than barely announced to the world, can perform what Christianity in eighteen hundred years has failed to do.

They must not expect any of these things have already been accomplished, but I will tell you what they may expect. They may expect more good to result from the perfect freedom which we advocate in one century than has resulted in a hundred centuries from all other causes, since the results will be in exact proportion to the extended application of the freedom. We have a legitimate right to predicate such results, since all freedom that has been practiced in all ages of the world has been beneficial just in proportion to the extent of human nature it covered.

Will any of you dare to stand up and assert that Religious Freedom ever produced a single bad result? or that Political Freedom ever injured a single soul who embraced and practiced it? If you can do so, then you may legitimately assert that Social Freedom may also produce equally bad results, but you cannot do otherwise, and be either conscientious or honest.

It is too late in the age for intelligent people to cry out thief, unless they have first been robbed, and it is equally late for them to succeed in crying down anything as of the devil to which name attaches that angels love. It may be very proper and legitimate, and withal perfectly consistent, for philosophers of the Tribune school to bundle all the murderers, robbers and rascals together, and hand them over to our camp, labeled as Free Lovers. We will only object that they ought to hand the whole of humanity over, good, bad and indifferent, and not assort its worst representatives.

My friends, you see this thing we call Freedom is large word, implying a deal more than people have ever yet been able to recognize. It reaches out its all-embracing arms, and while encircling our good friends and neighbors, does not neglect to also include their less worthy brothers and sisters, every one of whom is just as much entitled to the use of this freedom as is either one of us.

But objectors tell us that freedom is a dangerous thing to have, and that they must be its conservators, dealing it out to such people, and upon such matters, as they shall appoint. Having coined our name, they straightway proceed to define it, and to give force to their definition, set about citing illustrations to prove not only their definition to be a true one, but also that its application is just.

Among the cases cited as evidences of the evil tendencies of Free Love are those of Richardson and Crittenden. The celebrated McFarland-Richardson case was heralded world-wide as a case of this sort. So far as Richardson and Mrs. McFarland were concerned, I have every reason to believe it was a genuine one, in so far as the preventing obstacles framed by the "conservators" would permit. But when they assert that the murder of Richardson by McFarland was the legitimate result of Free Love, then I deny it in toto. McFarland murdered Richardson because he believed that the law had sold Abby Sage soul and body to him, and, consequently, that he owned her, and that no other person had any right to her favor, and that she had no right to bestow her love upon any other person, unless that ownership was first satisfied. The murder of Richardson, then, is not chargeable to his love or her love, but to the fact of the supposed ownership, which right of possession the law of marriage conferred on McFarland.

If anything further is needed to make the reputation of that charge clear, I will give it by illustration. Suppose that a pagan should be converted to Christianity through the efforts of some Christian minister, and that the remaining pagans should kill that minister for what he had done, would the crime be chargeable upon the Christian religion? Will any of you make that assertion? If not, neither can you charge that the death of Richardson should be charged to Free Love. But a more recent case is still clearer proof of the correctness of my position. Mrs. Fair killed Crittenden. Why? Because she believed in the spirit of the marriage law; that she had a better right to him than had Mrs. Crittenden, to whom the law had granted him; and rather than to give him up to her, to whom he evidently desired to go, and where, following his right to freedom, he did go, she killed him. Could a more perfect case of the spirit of the marriage law be formulate? Most assuredly, no!

Now, from the standpoint of marriage, reverse this case to that of Free Love, and see what would have been the result had all those parties been believers in and practicers of that theory. When Mr. Crittenden evinced a desire to return to Mrs. Crittenden, Mrs. Fair, in practicing the doctrine of Free Love, would have said, "I have no right to you, other than you freely give; you loved me and exercised your right of freedom in so doing. You now desire to return to Mrs. Crittenden, which is equally your right, and which I must respect. Go, and in peace, and my blessing shall follow, and if it can return you to happiness, then will you be happy."

Would not that have been the better the Christian course, and would not every soul in the broad land capable of a noble impulse, and having knowledge of all the relevant facts, have honored Mrs. Fair for it? Instead of a murder, with the probability of another to complement it, would not all parties have been happy in having done right? Would not Mrs. Crittenden have even loved Mrs. Fair for such an example of nobility, and could she not safely have received her even into her own heart and home, and have been a sister to her, instead of the means of her conviction of murder?

I tell you, my friends and my foes, that you have taken hold of the wrong end of this business. You are shouldering upon Free Love the results that flow from precisely its antithesis, which is the spirit, if not the letter, of your marriage theory, which is slavery, and not freedom.

I have a better right to speak, as one having authority in this matter, than most of you have, since it has been my province to study it in all its various lights and shades. When I practiced clairvoyance, hundreds, aye thousands, of desolate, heart-broken men, as well as women, came to me for advice. And they were from all walks of life, from the humblest daily laborer to the haughtiest dame of wealth. The tales of horror, of wrongs in inflicted and endured, which were poured into my ears, first awakened me to a realization of the hollowness and the rottenness of society, and compelled me to consider whether laws which were prolific of so much crime and misery as I found to exist should be continued; and to ask the question whether it were not better to let the bond go free. In time I was fully convinced that marriage laws were productive of precisely the reverse of that for which they are supposed to have been framed, and I came to recommend the grant of entire freedom to those who were complained of an inconstant; and the frank asking for it by those who desired it. My invariable advice was: "Withdraw lovingly, but completely, all claim and all complaint as an injured and deserted husband or wife. You need not perhaps disguise the fact that you suffer keenly from it, but take on yourself all the fault that you have not been able to command a more continuous love; that you have not proved to be all that you once seemed to be. Show magnanimity, and in order to show it, try to feel it. Cultivate that kind of love which loves the happiness and well-being of your partner most, his or her person next, and yourself last. Be kind to, and sympathize with, the new attraction rather than waspish and indignant. Know for a certainty that love cannot be clutched or gained by being fought for; while it is not impossible that it may be won back by the nobility of one's own deportment. If it cannot be, then it is gone forever, and you must make the best of it and reconcile yourself to it, and do the next thing-you may perhaps continue to hold on to a slave, but you have lost a lover."

Some may indeed think if I can keep the semblance of a husband or wife, even if it be not a lover, better still that it be so. Such is not my philosophy or my faith, and for such I have no advice to give. I address myself to such as have souls, and whose souls are in question; if you belong to the other sort, take advice of a Tombs lawyer and not of me. I have seen a few instances of the most magnanimous action among the persons involved in a knot of love, and with the most angelic results. I believe that the love which goes forth to bless, and if it be to surrender in order to bless, is love in the true sense, and that it tends greatly to beget love, and that the love which is demanding thinking only of self, is not love.

I have learned that the first great error married people commit is in endeavoring to hide from each other the little irregularities into which all are liable to fall. Nothing is so conducive to continuous happiness as mutual confidence. In whom, if not in the husband or the wife, should be one confide? Should they not be each other's best friends, never failing in time of anxiety, trouble and temptation to give disinterested and unselfish counsel? From such a perfect confidence as I would have men and women cultivate, it is impossible that bad or wrong should flow. On the contrary, it is the only condition in which love and happiness can go hand in hand. It is the only practice that can insure continuous respect, without which love withers and dies out. Can you not see that in mutual confidence and freedom the very strongest bonds of love are forged? It is more blessed to grant favors than to demand them, and the blessing is large and prolific of happiness, or small and insignificant in results, just in proportion as the favor granted is large or small. Tried by this rule, the greater the blessing or happiness you can confer on your partners, in which your own selfish feelings are not consulted, the greater the satisfaction that will redound to yourself. Think of this mode of adjusting your difficulties, and see what a clear way opens before you. There are none who have once felt the influence of a high order of love, so callous, but that they intuitively recognize the true grandeur and nobility of such a line of conduct. It must always be remembered that you can never do right until you are first free to do wrong; since the doing of a thing under compulsion is evidence neither of good nor bad intent; and if under compulsion, who shall decide what would be the substituted rule of action under full freedom?

In freedom alone is there safety and happiness, and when people learn this great fact, they will have just begun to know how to live. Instead then of being the destroying angel of the household, I would become the angel of purification to purge out all insincerity, all deception, all baseness and all vice, and to replace them by honor, confidence and truth.

I know very well that much of the material upon which the work must begin is very bad and far gone in decay. But I would have everybody perfectly free to do either right or wrong according to the highest standard, and if there are those so unfortunate as not to know how to do that which can alone bring happiness, I would treat them as we treat those who are intellectual without culture- who are ignorant and illiterate. There are none so ignorant but they may be taught. So, too, are there none so unfortunate in their understanding of the true and high relation of the sexes as not to be amenable to the right kind of instruction. First of all, however, the would- be teachers of humanity must become truly Christian, meek and lowly in spirit, forgiving and kind in action, and ever ready to do as did Christ to the Magdalen. We are not so greatly different from what the accusing multitude were in that time. But Christians, forgetting the teaching of Christ, condemn and say, "Go on in your sin." Christians must learn to claim nothing for themselves that they are unwilling to accord others. They must remember that all people endeavor, so far as lies in their power, and so far as it is possible for them to judge, to exercise their human right, or determine what their action shall be, that will bring them most happiness; and instead of being condemned and cast out of society therefor, they should be protected therein, so long as others' rights are not infringed upon. We think they do not do the best thing; it is our duty to endeavor to show them the better and the higher, and to induce them to walk therein. But because a person chooses to perform an act that we think a bad one, we have no right to put the brand of excommunication upon him. It is our Christian and brotherly duty to persuade him instead that it is more to his good to do something better next time, at the same time, however, assuring him he only did what he had a right to do.

If our sisters who inhabit Greene street and other filthy localities choose to remain in debauch, and if our brothers choose to visit them there, they are only exercising the same right that we exercise in remaining away, and we have no more right to abuse and condemn them for exercising their rights that way, than they have to abuse and condemn us for exercising our rights our way. But we have a duty , and that is by our love, kindness and sympathy to endeavor to prevail upon them to desert those ways which we feel are so damaging to all that is high and pure and true in the relations of the sexes.

If these are the stray sheep from the fold of truth and purity, should we not go out and gather them in, rather than remain within the fold and hold the door shut, lest they should enter in and defile the fold? Nay, my friends, we have only an assumed right to thus sit in judgment over our unfortunate sisters, which is the same right of which men have made use to prevent women from participation in government.

The sin of all time has been the exercise of assumed powers. This is the essence of tyranny. Liberty is a great lesson to learn. It is a great step to vindicate our own freedom. It is more, far more, to learn to leave others free, and free to do just what we perhaps may deem wholly wrong. We must recognize that others have consciences and judgment and rights as well as we, and religiously abstain from the effort to make them better by the use of any means to which we have no right to resort, and to which we cannot resort without abridging the great doctrine, the charter of all our liberties, the doctrine of Human Rights.

But the public press, either in real or affected ignorance or what they speak, denounce Free Love as the justification of, and apologist for, all manner and kind of sexual debauchery, and thus, instead of being the teachers of the people, as they should be, are the power which inculcates falsehood and wrong. The teachings of Christ, whom so many now profess to imitate, were direct and simple upon this point. He was not too good to acknowledge all men as brothers and all women as sisters; it mattered not whether they were highly advanced in knowledge and morals, or if they were of low intellectual and moral culture.

It is seriously to be doubted if any of Christ's disciples, or men equally as good as were they, could gain fellowship in any of your Fifth avenue church palaces, since they were nothing more than the humblest of fishermen, of no social or mental standing. Nevertheless, they were quite good enough for Christ to associate with, and fit to be appointed by Him to be "fishers of men." The Church seems to have forgotten that good does sometimes come out of the Nazareths of the world, and that wisdom may fall from the mouths of "babes and sucklings." Quite too much of the old pharisaical spirit exists in society to-day to warrant its members' claims, that they are the representatives and followers of Christ. For they are the I-am-holier-than-thou kind of people, who affect to, and to a great extent do, prescribe the standards of public opinion, and who ostracise everybody who will not bow to their mandates.

Talk of Freedom, of equality, of justice! I tell you there is scarcely a thought put in practice that is worthy to be the offspring of those noble words. The veriest systems of despotism still reign in all matters pertaining to social life. Caste stands as boldly out in this country as it does in political life in the kingdoms of Europe.

It is true that we are obliged to accept the situation just as it is. If we accord freedom to all persons we must expect them to make their own best use thereof, and, as I have already said, must protect them in such use until they learn to put it to better uses. But in our predication we must be consistent, and now ask who among you would be worse men and women all social laws repealed?

Would you necessarily dissolve your present relations, desert your dependent husbands-for there are even some of them-and wives and children simply because you have the right so to do? You are all trying to deceive yourselves about this matter. Let me ask of husbands if they think there would be fifty thousand women of the town supported by them if their wives were ambitious to have an equal number of men of the town to support, and for the same purposes? I tell you, nay! It is because men are held innocent of this support, and all the vengeance is visited upon the victims, that they have come to have an immunity in their practices.

Until women come to hold men to equal account as they do the women with whom they consort; or until they regard these women as just as respectable as the men who support them, society will remain in its present scale of moral excellence. A man who is well known to have been the constant visitor to these women is accepted into society, and if he be rich is eagerly sought both by mothers having marriageable daughters and by the daughters themselves. But the women with whom they have consorted are too vile to be even acknowledged as worthy of Christian burial, to say nothing of common Christian treatment. I have heard women reply when this difficulty was pressed upon them, "We cannot ostracise men as we are compelled to women, since we are dependent on them for support. " Ah! here's the rub. But do you not see that these other sisters are also dependent upon men for their support, and mainly so because you render it next to impossible for them to follow any legitimate means of livelihood? And are only those who have been fortunate enough to secure legal support entitled to live?

When I hear that argument advanced, my heart sinks

within me at the degraded condition of my sisters. They submit to a degradation simply because they see no alternative except self-support, and they see no means for that. To put on the semblance of holiness they cry out against those who, for like reasons, submit to like degradation; the only difference between the two being in a licensed ceremony, and a slip of printed paper costing twenty-five cents and upward.

The good women of one of the interior cities of New York some two years since organized a movement to put down prostitution. They were, by stratagem, to find out who visited houses of prostitution, and then were to ostracise them. They pushed the matter until they found their own husbands, brothers and sons involved, and then suddenly desisted, and nothing has since been heard of the eradication of prostitution in that city. If the same experiment were to be tried in New York the result would be the same. The supporters of prostitution would be found to be those whom women cannot ostracise. The same disability excuses the presence of women in the very home, and I need not tell you that Mormonism is practice in other places beside Utah. But what is the logic of these things? Why, simply this, A woman, be she wife or mistress, who consorts with a man who consorts with other women, is equally, with them and him, morally responsible, since the receiver is held to be as culpable as the thief.

The false and hollow relations of the sexes are thus resolved into the mere question of the dependence of women upon men for support, and women, whether married or single, are supported by men because they are women and their opposites in sex. I can see no moral difference between a woman who marries and lives with a man because he can provide for her wants, and the woman who is not married, but who is provided for at the same price. There is a legal difference, to be sure, upon one side of which is set the seal of respectability, but there is no virtue in law. In the fact of law, however, is the evidence of the lack of virtue, since if the law be required to enforce virtue, its real presence is wanting; and women need to comprehend this truth.

The sexual relation, must be rescued from this insidious form of slavery. Women must rise from their position as ministers to the passions of men to be their equals. Their entire system of education must be changed. They must be trained to be like men, permanent and independent individualities, and not their mere appendages or adjuncts, with them forming but one member of society. They must be the companions of men from choice, never from necessity.

It is a label upon nature and God to say this world is not calculated to make women, equally with men, self-reliant and self-supporting individuals. In present customs, however, this is apparently impossible. There must come a change, and one of the direct steps to it will be found in the newly claimed political equality of women with men. This attained, one degree of subjugation will be removed. Next will come, following equality of right, equality of duty, which includes the duty of self-hood, or independence as an individual. Nature is male and female throughout, and each sex is equally dependent upon nature for sustenance. It is an infamous thing to say a condition of society which requires women to enter into and maintain sexual relations with men is their legitimate method of protecting life. Sexual relations should be the result of entirely different motives that for the purpose of physical support. The spirit of the present theory is, that they are entered upon and maintained as a means of physical gratification, regardless of the consequences which may result therefrom, and are administered by the dictum of the husband, which is often in direct opposition to the will and wish of the wife. She has no control over her own person, having been taught to "submit herself to her husband."

I protest against this form of slavery, I protest against the custom which compels women to give the control of their maternal functions over to anybody. It should be theirs to determine when, and under what circumstances, the greatest of all constructive processes-the formation of an immoral soul-should be begun. It is a fearful responsibility with which women are intrusted by nature, and the very last thing that they should be compelled to do is to perform the office of that responsibility against their will, under improper conditions or by disgusting means.

What can be more terrible than for a delicate, sensitively organized woman to be compelled to endure the presence of a beast in the shape of a man, who knows nothing beyond the blind passion with which he is filled, and to which is often added to delirium of intoxication? You do not need to be informed that there are many persons who, during the acquaintance preceding marriage, preserve a delicacy, tenderness and regard for womanly sensitiveness and modest refinement which are characteristic of true women, thus winning and drawing out their love-nature to the extreme, but who, when the decree has been pronounced which makes them indissolubly theirs, cast all these aside and reveal themselves in their true character, as without regard, human or divine, for aught save their own desires. I know I speak the truth, and you too know I speak the truth, when I say that thousands of the most noble, loving-natured women by whom the world was ever blessed, prepared for, and desirous of pouring their whole life into the bond of union, prophesied by marriage, have had all these generous and warm impulses thrust back upon them by the rude monster into which the previous gentleman developed. To these natures thus frosted and stultified in their fresh youth and vigor, life becomes a burden almost too terrible to be borne, and thousands of pallid checks, sunken eyes, distorted imaginations and diseased functions testify too directly and truly to leave a shade of doubt as to their real cause. Yet women, in the first instance, and men through them as their mothers, with an ignorant persistence worthy only of the most savage despotism, seem determined that it shall not be investigated; and so upon this voluntary ignorance and willful persistence society builds. It is high time, however, that they should be investigated, high time that your sisters and daughters should no longer be led to the altar like sheep to the shambles, in ignorance of the uncertainties they must inevitably encounter. For it is no slight thing to hazard a life's happiness upon a single act.

I deem it a false and perverse modesty that shuts off

discussion, and consequently knowledge, upon these subjects. They are vital, and I never performed a duty which I felt more called upon to perform than I now do in denouncing as barbarous the ignorance which is allowed to prevail among young women about to enter those relations which, under present customs, as often bring a life-long misery as happiness.

Mistakes made in this most important duty of life can never be rectified; a commentary upon the system which of itself is sufficient in the sight of common sense to forever condemn it. In marriage, however, common sense is dispensed with, and a usage substituted therefor which barbarism has bequeathed us, and which becomes more barbarous as the spiritual natures of women gain the ascendancy over the mere material. The former slaves, before realizing that freedom was their God-appointed right, did not feel the horrors of their condition. But when, here and there, some among them began to have an interior knowledge that they were held in obedience by an unrighteous power, they then began to rebel in their souls. So, too, is it with women. So long as they knew nothing beyond a blind and servile obedience and perfect self-abnegation to the will and wish of men, they did not rebel; but the time has arrived wherein, here and there, a soul is awakened by some terrible ordeal, or some divine inspiration, to the fact that women as much as men are personalities, responsible to themselves for the use which they permit to be made of themselves, and they rebel demanding freedom, to hold their own lives and bodies from the demoralizing influence of sexual relations that are not founded in and maintained by love. And this rebellion will continue, too, until love, unshackled, shall be free to go to bless the object that can call it forth, and until, when called forth, it shall be respected as holy, pure and true. Every day farther and wider does it spread, and bolder does it speak. None too soon will the yoke fall by which the unwilling are made to render a hypocritical obedience to the despotism of public opinion, which, distorted and blinded by a sham sentimentality, is a false standard of morals and virtue, and which is utterly destructive to true morality and to real virtue, which can only be fostered and cultivated by freedom of the affections.

Free Love, then, is the law by which men and women of all grades and kinds are attracted to or repelled from each other, and does not describe the results accomplished by either; these results depend upon the condition and development of the individual subjects. It is the natural operation of the affectional motives of the sexes, unbiased by any enacted law or standard of public opinion. It is the opportunity which gives the opposites in sex the conditions in which the law of chemical affinities raised into the domain of the affections can have unrestricted sway, as it has in all departments of nature except in enforced sexual relations among men and women.

It is an impossibility to compel incompatible elements of matter to unite. So also is it impossible to compel incompatible elements of human nature to unite. The sphere of chemical science is to bring together such elements as will produce harmonious compounds. The sphere of social science is to accomplish the same thing in humanity. Anything that stands in the way of this accomplishment in either department is an obstruction to the natural order of the universe. There would be just as much common sense for the chemist to write a law commanding that two incompatible elements should unite, or that two, once united, should so remain, even if a third, having a stronger affinity for one of them than they have for each other, should be introduced, as it is for chemists of society to attempt to do the same by individuals; for both are impossible. If in chemistry two properties are united by which the environment is not profited, it is the same law of affinity which operates as where a compound is made that is of the greatest service to society. This law holds in social chemistry; the results obtained from social compounds will be just such as their respective properties determine.

Thus I might go on almost infinitely to illustrate the difference which must be recognized between the operations of a law and the law itself. Now the whole difficulty in marriage law is that it endeavors to compel unity between elements in which it is impossible; consequently there is an attempt made to subvert not only the general order of the universe, but also the special intentions of nature, which are those of God. The results, then, flowing from operations of the law of Free Love will be high, pure and lasting, or low, debauched and promiscuous, just in the degree that those loving, are high or low in the scale of sexual progress; while each and all are strictly natural, and therefore legitimate in their respective spheres.

Promiscuity in sexuality is simply the anarchical stage of development wherein the passions rule supreme. When spirituality comes in and rescues the real man or woman from the domain of the purely material, promiscuity is simply impossible. As promiscuity is the analogue to anarchy, so is spirituality to scientific selection and adjustment. Therefore I am fully persuaded that the very highest sexual unions are those that are monogamic, and that these are perfect in proportion as they are lasting. Now if to this be added the fact that the highest kind of love is that which is utterly freed from and devoid of selfishness, and whose highest gratification comes from rendering its object the greatest amount of happiness, let that happiness depend upon whatever it may, then you have my ideal of the highest order of love and the most perfect degree of order to which humanity can attain. An affection that does not desire to bless its object, instead of appropriating it by a selfish possession to its own uses, is not worthy the name of love. Love is that which exists to do good, not merely to get good, which is constantly giving instead of desiring.

A Csar is admired by humanity, but a Christ is revered. These persons who have lived and sacrificed themselves most for the good of humanity, without thought of recompense, are held in greatest respect. Christian believes that Christ died to save the world, giving His life as a ransom therefor. That was the greatest gift He could make to show His love for mankind.

The general test of love to-day is entirely different from that which Christ gave. That is now deemed the greatest love which has the strongest and most uncontrollable wish to be made happy, by the appropriation, and if need be the sacrifice, of all the preferences of its objects. It says:

"Be mine. Whatever may be your wish, yield it up to me." How different would the world be were this sort of selfishness supplanted by the Christ love, which says: Let this cup pass from me. Nevertheless, not my will but thine be done. Were the relations of the sexes thus regulated, misery, crime and vice would be banished, and the pale, wan face of female humanity replaced by one glowing with radiant delight and healthful bloom, and the heart of humanity beat with a heightened vigor and renewed strength, and its intellect cleared of all shadows, sorrows and blights. Contemplate this, and then denounce me for advocating Freedom if you can, and I will bear your curse with a better resignation.

Oh! my brothers and sisters, let me entreat you to have more faith in the self-regulating efficacy of freedom. Do you not see how beautifully it works among us in other respects? In America everybody is free to worship God according to the dictates of his own conscience, or even not to worship anything, notwithstanding you or I may think that very wicked or wrong. The respect for freedom we make paramount over our individual opinions, and the result is peace and harmony, when the people of other countries are still throttling and destroying each other to enforce their individual opinions on others. Free Love is only the appreciation of this beautiful principle of freedom. One step further I entreat you to trust it still, and though you may see a thousand dangers, I see peace and happiness and steady improvement as the result.

To more specifically define Free Love I would say that I prefer to use the word love with lust as its antithesis, love representing the spiritual and lust the animal; the perfect and harmonious interrelations of the two being the perfected human. This use has its justification in other pairs of words; as good and evil; heat and cold; light and dark; up and down; north and south; which in principle are the same, but in practice we are obliged to judge of them as relatively different. The point from which judgment is made is that which we occupy, or are related to, individually, at any given time. Thus what would be up to one person might be down to another differently situated, along the line which up and down described. So also is it of good and evil. What is good to one low down the ladder may not only be, but actually is, evil to one further ascended; nevertheless it is the same ladder up which both climb. It is the comprehension of this scientific fact that guarantees the best religion. And it is the non-comprehension of it that sets us as judges of our brothers and sisters, who are below us in the scale of development, to whom we should reach down the kind and loving hand of assistance, rather than force them to retreat farther away from us by unkindness, denunciation and hate.

In fine, and to resume: We have found that humanity is composed of men and women of all grades of developments, from the most hideous human monster up to the highest perfected saint: that all of them, under our theory of government, are entitled to worship God after the dictates of their several consciences; that God is worshiped just as essentially in political and social thought and action as He is in religious thought and action; that no second person or persons have any right to interfere with the action of the individual unless he interfere with others' rights, and then only to protect such rights; that the thoughts and actions of all individuals, whether high and pure, or low and debauched, are equally entitled to the protection of the laws, and, through them, to that of all members of the community. Religious thought and action already receive the equal protection of the laws. Political thought and action are about to secure the equal protection of the laws. What social thought and action demand of the laws and their administrators is the same protection which Religion has, and Politics is about to have.

I know full well how strong is the appeal that can be made in behalf of marriage, an appeal based on the sanctions of usage and inherited respect, and on the sanctions of religion reinforced by the sanctions of law. I know how much can be said, and how forcibly it can be said, on the ground that women, and especially that the children born of the union of the sexes, must be protected, and must, therefore, have the solemn contract of the husband and father to that effect. I know how long and how powerfully the ideality and sentiment of mankind have clustered, as it were in a halo, around this time-honored institution of marriage. And yet I solemnly believe that all that belongs to a dispensation of force and contract, and of a law and unworthy sense of mutual ownership, which is passing, and which is destined rapidly to pass, completely away; not to leaves us without love, nor without the happiness and beauty of the most tender relation of human souls; nor without security for woman, and ample protection for children; but to lift us to a higher level in the enjoyment of every blessing. I believe in love with liberty; in protection without slavery; in the care and culture of offspring by new and better methods, and without the tragedy of self-immolation on the part of parents. I believe in the family, spiritually constituted, expanded, amplified, and scientifically and artistically organized, as a unitary home. I believe in the most wonderful transformation of human society as about to come, as even now at the very door, through general progress, science and the influential intervention of the spirit world. I believe in more than all that the millennium has ever signified to the most religious mind; and I believe that in order to prepare minds to contemplate and desire and enact the new and better life, it is necessary that the old and still prevalent superstitious veneration for the legal marriage tie be relaxed and weakened; not to pander to immorality, but as introductory to a nobler manhood and a more glorified womanhood; as, indeed, the veritable gateway to a paradise regained.

Do not criticize me, therefore, from a commonplace point of view. Question me, first, of the grounds of my faith. Conceive, if you can, the outlook for that humanity which comes trooping through the long, bright vista of futurity, as seen by the eyes of a devout spiritualist and a transcendental socialist. My whole nature is prophetic. I do not and cannot live merely in the present. Credit, first, the burden of my prophecy; and from the new standing-ground so projected forth into the future, look back upon our times, and so judge of my doctrine; and if, still, you cannot concede either the premises or the conclusion, you may, perhaps, think more kindly of me personally, as an amiable enthusiast, than if you deemed me deliberately wicked in seeking to disturb the foundations of our existing social order.

I prize dearly the good opinion of my fellow-beings. I would. so gladly, have you think well of me, and not ill. It is because I love you all, and love your well-being still more than I love you, that I tell you my vision of the future, and that I would willingly disturb your confidence, so long cherished, in the old dead or dying-out past. Believe me honest, my dear friends, and so forgive and think of me lovingly in turn, even if you are compelled still to regard me as deceived. I repeat, that I love you all; that I love every human creature, and their well being; and that I believe, with the profoundest conviction, that what I have urged in this discourse is conducive to that end.

Thus have I explained to you what Social Freedom or, as some choose to denominate it, Free Love, is, and what its advocates demand. Society says, to grant it is to precipitate itself into anarchy. I oppose to this arbitrary assumption the logic of general freedom, and aver that order and harmony will be secured where anarchy now reigns. The order of nature will soon determine whether society is or I am right. Let that be as it may, I repeat: "The love that I cannot command is not mine; let me not disturb myself about it, nor attempt to filch it from its rightful owner. A heart that I supposed mine has drifted and gone. Shall I go in pursuit? Shall I forcibly capture the truant and transfix it with the barb of my selfish affection, and pin it to the wall of my character? Rather let me leave my doors and windows open, intent only on living so nobly that the best cannot fail to be drawn to me by an irresistible attraction."

THE NEW ERA

Almost simultaneously with the enunciation of the Principles of Social Freedom, in other words, the Natural Laws which underlie the Social Relations of the Sexes, comes the voice of Alfred Tennyson from beyond the seas. Harper's Weekly, the journal of civilization, gives us his last utterance, "The Last Tournament." In the Poet Laureate's melodious lines we find the rhythmical echo of those solemn and all-important truths which we had put forward in ruder but not less earnest prose. That the Harpers should publish truths in poetry which they denounce in prose does not surprise us. The form and manner of the utterance make such a difference; the renown of the prophet insures an audience; publishers are mortal. With them it is not the doctrine, but its pecuniary acceptableness. Does it pay? But we wait with wonder to see what the press shall say of this newest proclamation, "by authority," of self-evident truths. The "bald and bold" pronunciamento of Steinway Hall is overlaid by the subtle refinements and pure elegance of the most sentimental and most philosophic poet of the age. We are denounced as wishing to reduce the sexual relation to simple promiscuity, while our faith and our contention are that perfect freedom would annihilate all temptation to promiscuity. We denounce promiscuity and licentiousness with all our might, and shall protest against them to our latest breath. Let Sir Tristram speak for us:

"The vow that binds too strictly snaps itself,

103

We run more counter to the soul thereof
Than had we never sworn"-

We shall be glad to hear what our supersanctified, self-approved judges, who condemn us to the lowest Tophet, shall say of Tennyson for his definitions of Freedom without any discrimination of phase or person. What will they say of the good Harpers for publishing such infidelity and immorality-

"Good now, what have I broken, fool?"
And little Dagnonet, skipping, "Arthur, the King's;
For when thou playest that air with Queen Isolt,
Chou makest broken music with thy bride,
Her daintier namesake down in Brittany-
And so thou breakest Arthur's music too."
"Save for that broken music in thy brains,
Sir Fool," said Tristam, "I would break thy head.
Fool, I came late, the heathen wars were o'er,
The life had flown, we sware but by the shell-
I am but a fool to reason with a fool-
Come,thou art crabb'd and sour; but lean me down,
Sir Dagonet, one of thy long asses' ears,
And hearken if my music be not true.

" Free love-free field-we love but while we may:
The woods are hush'd, their music is no more:
The leaf is dead, the yearning past away:
New leaf, new life-the days of frost are o'er:
New life, new love to suit the newer day:
New loves are sweet as those that went before:
Free love-free field-we love but while we may.

"Ye might have moved slow-measure to my tune,
No stood stockstill. I made if in the woods,
And found if ring as true as tested gold."

Then Tristam, pacing moodily up and down,
"Vows! did ye keep the vow ye made to Mark
More than I mine! Lied, say ye? Nay, but learnt,
The vow that binds too strictly snaps itself-
My knighthood taught me this-ay, being snapt-
We run more counter to the soul thereof
Than had we never sworn . I swear no more.
I swore to the great King, and am forsworn.
For once-ev'n to the height-I honor'd him.
Man, is he man at all?

"He seem'd to me no man,
But Michael trampling Satan; so I sware,
Being amazed: but this went by -the vows!
O ay-the wholesome madness of an hour-
They served their use;
"But then their vows-
First mainly thro' that sallying of our Queen-
Began to call the knighthood, asking whence

Had Arthur right to bind them to himself?
To bind them by inviolable vows,
Which flesh and blood perforce would violate:
Can Arthur make me pure
As any maiden child? lock up my tongue
From uttering freely what I freely hear?
Bindme to one? The great world laughs at it.
And worldling of the world am I, and know
The ptarmigan that whitens ere his hour

Wooes his own end; we are not angels here
Nor shall be: vows-woodman of the woods,
And hear the garnet-headed yaffingale
Mock them: my soul, we love but while we may,
And therefore is my love so large for thee,
Seeing it is not bounded save by love."

Here ending, he moved toward her, and she said,
"Good: and I turn'd away my love for thee
To some one thrice as courteous as thyself-
For courtesy wins woman all as well
As valor may-but he that closes both
Is perfect, he is Lancelot-taller indeed,
Roster and comelier, thou-but say I loved
This knightliest of all knights, and cast thee back
Thine own small saw, We love but while we may,
Well, then, what answer?"

He that while she spake
Mindful of what he brought to adorn her with,
The jewels, had let one finger lightly touch
The warm white apple of her throat, replied,
"Press this a little closer, sweet, until-
Come, I am hunger'd and half anger'd-meat,
Wine, wine-and I will love thee to the death,
And out beyond into the dream to come."
So then, when both were brought to full accord,
She rose, and set before him all he will'd;
And after these had comforted the blood
With meats and wines, and satiated their hearts-
Now talking of their woodland paradise,
The deer, the dews, the fern, the founts, the lawns;
Now mocking at the much ungainliness,

And craven shifts, and long crane legs of Mark-
Then Tristam laughing caught the harp, and sang:
"Ay, ay, O ay-the winds that bend the brier!
A star in heaven, a star within the mere!
Ay, ay, O ay-a star was my desire;
And one was far apart, and one was near:
Ay, ay, O ay-the winds that bow the grass!
And one was water and one star was fire,
And one will ever shine and one will pass-
Ay, ay, O ay-the winds that move the mere."

www.ingramcontent.com/pod-product-compliance
Lightning Source LLC
Chambersburg PA
CBHW021934040426
42448CB00008B/1062